TYMURS

The 1982 Tylenol Murders

(TYMURS, Book 1)

SCOTT BARTZ

New Light Publishing

Cover designed by Derek Murphy of Creativindie Covers

ISBN-13: 978-1475000849

ISBN-10: 1475000847

CONTENTS

1

A Premonition

It was shaping up to be a banner year for Johnson & Johnson when the corporation's top executives met on September 7, 1982 for their annual three-day strategic planning review. The company was in the midst of a long run of steady earnings growth. But James Burke, J&J's chairman and chief executive officer, was worried that some future problem might threaten the company's strong financial position.

"I took some kidding at that meeting for worrying about things I don't have to," Burke recalled later. "We had been marveling at how lucky we were to be in our industry, to have some very profitable brands doing so well, and I had said, offhand, what if something happens to one of them, like Tylenol?"

The company that manufactured and sold Tylenol—the McNeil consumer Products Company—was led by Wayne Nelson, the company's co-founder and chairman. However, during the September planning review, Nelson was appointed vice president of J&J International, and David Collins took over as the chairman of McNeil. Collins, who had grown up in the Chicago suburb of Oak Park, Illinois, was in his new position for just three weeks when a harbinger of the coming "Tylenol crisis" unfolded 32 miles northwest of his boyhood home.

*****

Deputy Joseph Chavez pulled into the parking lot at the Howard Johnson's Motor Lodge and Restaurant in Elgin, Illinois on the morning of Tuesday, September 28, 1982. He was joined a minute later by Deputy Al Swanson. The deputies, working the

1

midnight to 8 a.m. shift for the Kane County Sheriff's Department, were meeting at the all-night restaurant for breakfast.

Swanson and Chavez exited their vehicles at 2:32 a.m. As they headed toward the restaurant's entrance, Chavez noticed two cardboard boxes resting on the pavement next to the grass median that ran between the parking lot and Route 25. The labels on the boxes gradually came into focus as the deputies walked toward them. The words "EXTRA-STRENGTH TYLENOL CAPSULES" were embossed in bold uppercase letters on the right half of each box-front. On the left half, the Tylenol manufacturer's name, "McNEIL," was imprinted just above the description of the contents: twelve 6-packs of 50-count bottles of Extra Strength Tylenol capsules.

One of the boxes was open. Two dozen Tylenol bottles remained in the open box, and two of those bottles were also open. Strewn on the pavement within a few feet of the boxes were hundreds of red and white capsule-parts labeled with the 500-milligram Extra Strength Tylenol dosage mark. In between the boxes was "a big pile of powder that looked as if it had been dumped."

"It looked like hundreds of capsules had been emptied," Chavez said later. "We looked at them and found a couple of capsules that had been put back together."

Chavez picked up and examined a few of the capsules and capsule-parts and then tossed them back onto the ground. Unconcerned about what they had found, the deputies went into the restaurant, grabbed a booth, and ordered breakfast. As they ate, Chavez developed a headache and a strange, painful rash and swelling on his arm. The deputies finished breakfast and walked back out to their cars, stopping along the way to take another look at the Tylenol capsules.

Deputy Swanson picked up a few of the capsules and then scraped up some of the white powder and rubbed it between his fingers. He guessed that the capsules may have been emptied by drug dealers who had planned to mix the acetaminophen with cocaine. Still, it was odd that some of the capsule-parts had been refilled and "put back together." The Tylenol 500mg labels on the reassembled capsules were misaligned as a result.

Swanson and Chavez got into their squad cars and drove off. Minutes later, however, Swanson pulled over to the side of the road when he suddenly became violently ill, with vomiting, a headache, and dizziness—all symptoms of cyanide poisoning, which can occur from inhalation or absorption through the skin.

Having made no immediate connection between the Tylenol capsules and the sudden onset of their mysterious illnesses, the deputies left the boxes of Extra Strength Tylenol capsules right where they had found them, sitting in the Howard Johnson's parking lot at the intersection of Route 25 and Interstate 90, about 38 miles northwest of Chicago.

2

Death without Warning

Sixteen hours after the Kane County deputies had stumbled upon the cases of Extra Strength Tylenol capsules, Jeanna Kellerman stood in the health and beauty care section of a Jewel-Osco store in Elk Grove Village, 19 miles east of Elgin Howard Johnson's. She scanned the shelves and then grabbed a bottle of Extra Strength Tylenol capsules. A store employee revealed later that the Tylenol display had been restocked the previous night.

The following morning, Wednesday, September 29, 1982, Jeanna's twelve-year-old daughter, Mary, awoke at about 7 a.m. with a sore throat and a cough. Mary's father, Dennis, got out of bed and walked down the hall to check on her. He told Mary that she should stay home from school for the day. Then he went into the bathroom, opened the medicine cabinet, and took out the bottle of Extra Strength Tylenol that Jeanna had purchased about 12 hours earlier. Dennis returned to Mary's bedroom and gave her one Tylenol capsule.

Dennis had just gotten back into bed when he heard Mary go into the bathroom and close the door. Then he heard something drop. Dennis walked back down the hall to the bathroom. "Mary, are you okay?" he asked. He got no response, so he asked again, "Mary, are you okay?" Then he opened the door and saw his daughter lying on the bathroom floor.

Mary was in full cardiac arrest when the ambulance arrived. The paramedics tried, unsuccessfully, to revive Mary at the house before rushing her to Alexian Brothers Medical Center in Elk Grove Village. Mary was pronounced dead at 10:00 a.m. from what the doctors could only guess at the time was an aneurism or a heart attack.

In nearby Arlington Heights, 27-year-old Adam Janus had taken the day off from his job at the Elk Grove Village Post Office. Adam had emigrated from Poland in 1970. He went back to Poland in 1975 to marry his sweetheart, Teresa, and together they had moved into a modest home in Arlington Heights.

Late Wednesday morning, Adam made a quick trip to the Jewel-Osco store on Vail Avenue in Arlington Heights. He bought a steak for dinner, some flowers for his wife, and a bottle of Extra Strength Tylenol capsules for himself. Adam returned home and had lunch with Teresa. He then swallowed two Extra Strength Tylenol capsules. He soon told Teresa that he wasn't feeling well and went into the bedroom to lie down for a while.

Teresa checked on Adam a few minutes later and found him unconscious and convulsing. She called the Arlington Heights Fire Department at about 2 p.m. When the paramedics arrived, Adam was unconscious, his breathing was labored, his blood pressure dangerously low, and his pupils fixed and dilated. Adam was taken to the emergency room at Northwest Community Hospital and pronounced dead at 3:15 p.m.

Dr. Thomas Kim, the medical director of the hospital's intensive care unit, met and spoke to Adam's parents, his wife, his brother Stanley, and Stanley's wife Theresa. He did not yet have an explanation for Adam's death. Later, when discussing his efforts to save Adam's life, Dr. Kim remarked, "Nothing seemed to help. He suffered sudden death without warning. It was most unusual."

Around the same time Adam was pronounced dead, 27-year-old Mary Magdalene Reiner, who went by the name "Lynn," was inside the Frank's Finer Foods store in Winfield, about 25 miles south of Arlington Heights. She had gone there to buy a bottle of Tylenol. Lynn had checked out of Central DuPage Hospital in Winfield the previous day after giving birth five days earlier to a baby boy. Lynn and her husband Ed had two daughters, Dawn and Michelle; a son, Jacob; and now a newborn, Joshua.

Lynn bought a bottle of Regular Strength Tylenol capsules at Frank's Finer Foods and returned home shortly before 3:30 p.m. She went into the living room where her mother-in-law was watching Joshua and her 21-month old son, Jacob. Lynn rummaged through the goodie-bag she'd been given at the hospital the previous day. She then took two Extra Strength Tylenol capsules—not the Regular Strength Tylenol capsules she had just bought. A few minutes later, Lynn told her mother-in-law that she felt nauseous. Lynn got up from the couch and walked into the kitchen on her way to the bathroom. Suddenly feeling very dizzy, she stopped and sat down on one of the kitchen chairs. Lynn's mother-in-law, realizing something was wrong, rushed to her side.

Outside, Ed had just pulled into the driveway, along with the Reiner's 8-year-old daughter, Michelle. They walked into the kitchen and entered what had now become a chaotic and frightening scene. Lynn was sitting at the table, her breathing was labored. Ed's mom ordered Ed to call an ambulance. Now frantic, Ed fumbled with the phone, dropped the receiver, then quickly snatched it back up and dialed the operator. As Ed instructed the operator to send an ambulance, Lynn fell to the floor and went into convulsions.

Winfield Police Officer Scott Watkins arrived at the Reiners' home at 3:45 p.m. He was followed moments later by emergency medical technicians from Leonard's Ambulance Service and the Winfield Fire Department. After working on Lynn at the house for several minutes, to no avail, the paramedics rushed her to Central DuPage Hospital.

Michelle's most vivid memories of that day are the sounds. She can still hear the thump of her mom hitting the floor, her mom's labored breathing, and the firm voice of her father commanding her to take the dog and go upstairs. She watched from her bedroom window as her mom was taken away in an ambulance, sirens blaring.

Shortly after Lynn was admitted to Central DuPage Hospital at 5 p.m., Mary McFarland was at work at the Bell Phone Center in Yorktown Mall in Lombard, ten miles east of Winfield, searching through her purse for a bottle containing Extra Strength Tylenol capsules. Mary told her co-workers that she'd been fighting a bad headache all day long. After finishing work the previous evening, Mary had walked to the Woolworth store in her mall and picked up a bottle of Extra Strength Tylenol capsules. When she got home that night, she dumped 17 capsules from her new 50-count bottle of Tylenol into a small Dristan bottle she kept in her purse. She had already consumed five of those Tylenol capsules, and now, in the store's break room, she took two more.

Mary soon began to feel nauseous and dizzy. She walked over to the break-room table where some of her co-workers were sitting. "I don't feel good, guys," she said, and then she fell forward onto the table. Her coworkers called an ambulance and Mary was taken to Good Samaritan Hospital in Downers Grove, arriving at 7:20 p.m. Doctors initially suspected that Mary, a 31-year-old divorced mother of two children, ages one and four, had died from an aneurism or a stroke.

Mary McFarland and Lynn Reiner were clinically dead within minutes of swallowing the cyanide-laced Tylenol capsules, but doctors resuscitated their hearts, and both were put on life support. Doctors at Good Samaritan Hospital took Mary off life support at 3:18 a.m. Thursday. Later that morning, a neurologist at Central DuPage Hospital disconnected the machines keeping Lynn alive and pronounced her dead at 9:05 a.m.

There were no apparent connections between the deaths of Mary Kellerman, Adam Janus, Mary McFarland, and Lynn Reiner. They had died in different towns, and the emergency calls were handled by paramedics and doctors from different townships. The coroners' offices in Cook and DuPage Counties, where the deaths occurred, did not test for cyanide in death cases unless specifically requested to do so. As the medical examiners had no reason to suspect foul play, they did not intend to investigate these deaths as murders or test the victims' blood for cyanide.

3

Maybe It's the Tylenol

Adam Janus's 24-year-old brother, Stanley, and Stanley's 19-year-old bride, Theresa, had left Northwest Community Hospital late Wednesday afternoon with Adam's now widow, Teresa, and went to her home in Arlington Heights. They entered the house and walked into the kitchen where the bottle of Extra Strength Tylenol was still sitting on the countertop. They all had been crying, and both Stanley and his wife Theresa had developed headaches. Stanley picked up the Tylenol bottle, dumped two of the red and white capsules into his hand and then popped them into his mouth. Theresa called her parents to deliver the sad news of her brother-in-law's death. After a short conversation, Theresa hung up the phone, and then she too picked up the Tylenol bottle, poured out two capsules, and swallowed them. Stanley brought the Tylenol bottle into the bathroom and placed it in the medicine cabinet. He returned to the kitchen and was about to go outside and smoke a cigarette when he fainted and went into convulsions.

Theresa called the Arlington Heights Fire Department at 6 p.m., and for the second time that day, paramedic Chuck Kramer and the Arlington Heights emergency team rushed to the Januses' house. While the emergency medical technicians worked on Stanley in the kitchen, Theresa, now panic-stricken, called her parents again—this time to tell them her husband was about to be taken to the hospital. Then, as Kramer watched in horror, Theresa collapsed onto the living room floor.

Dr. Kim, who had treated Adam Janus earlier in the day, was about to leave Northwest Community Hospital when he received the shocking news that Adam's brother and sister-in-law were being brought to the emergency room. Dr. Kim took off his jacket and waited for the ambulance to arrive.

The paramedics, despite their best efforts, could not keep the lives of Stanley and Theresa from slipping away, following the exact same pattern they had witnessed a few hours earlier while trying to revive Adam. When the ambulance arrived at the emergency room, Stanley and Theresa were in full cardiac arrest. The emergency room staff was able to get Theresa's heart beating again. They hooked her up to a respirator, but she had no brain activity.

While Dr. Kim continued his efforts to resuscitate Stanley, he went through a mental checklist, trying to figure out what could have happened to the Januses. He directed his staff to call several poison control centers. One minute later, Dr. John Sullivan, a poison expert at the Rocky Mountain Poison Center in Colorado, was on the line.

After listening to Dr. Kim described the Januses' symptoms, Dr. Sullivan said the symptoms sounded more like cyanide poisoning than anything else. Dr. Kim immediately directed his staff to find a local lab that could test blood samples for cyanide levels and to also contact someone from the public health department who could diagnose potential environmental hazards at the Janus home.

Helen Jensen, the Elk Grove Village public health nurse, was sitting down for a late dinner at home when the call came in from Northwest Community Hospital. The caller asked Helen to come to the hospital right away; she said something strange was going on.

Jensen left her half-eaten dinner and rushed to the hospital. When she arrived, the emergency staff was involved in an anxious discussion about what could have happened to the Januses. Helen looked around the emergency room and saw Adam's widow standing in the corner. Helen introduced herself and asked Teresa to describe the events leading up to the deaths. Teresa spoke only Polish, so with her brother-in-law acting as a translator, she told Helen everything she remembered about the incidents. Teresa said Adam, Stanley, and Theresa had all drank coffee and eaten peaches before they collapsed. They had also each taken Tylenol.

Helen knew she had to go to the Januses' house. Her co-workers, concerned that a gas leak or some other toxic substance inside the house might have poisoned the Januses, warned her to stay away. But Helen insisted on going anyway. She recruited a police officer to escort her to the Janus home. When they arrived at the house, Helen and the police officer searched the kitchen and found some used coffee grounds and a jar of peaches. Helen went into the bathroom and opened the medicine cabinet door. The bottle of Extra Strength Tylenol immediately caught her eye.

Helen brought the Tylenol bottle into the kitchen and then poured the capsules out onto the countertop. Helen and the police officer each counted the capsules. They each came up with the same number—44. *This has got to be it*, Helen thought. Six capsules were missing from the 50-count bottle, and three people taking the recommended dose of Tylenol would account for those missing capsules.

Jensen returned to the hospital with the coffee grounds, the peaches, and the Tylenol. "I knew in my heart that it had to be the Tylenol, but I couldn't get anyone to listen," she said later. "They pooh-poohed me."

Dr. Kim, however, had not yet ruled out any possible cause for the Januses' deaths. To make a proper diagnosis, he needed evidence—not a gut feeling. Dr. Kim opened the Januses' Tylenol bottle to make sure it contained only Tylenol capsules, which it did. He then called Cook County Medical Examiner Dr. Robert Stein, who was giving a lecture in Rockford, Illinois. Kim asked Stein and if he was aware of any new deadly recreational drug or suicidal cult (this was only three years after Reverend Jim Jones and his followers used cyanide to commit mass suicide). Stein was unaware of anything that might explain the sudden deaths of the Januses.

Meanwhile, Philip Cappitelli, an off-duty Arlington Heights firefighter, had been monitoring his police radio all day. Cappitelli heard the first ambulance call to the Janus house shortly after lunchtime. He was stunned when he heard the second call to the Janus home end with the same tragic outcome as the first call. Cappitelli now also became suspicious about the death of Mary Kellerman, which his mother-in-law had told him about that morning.

Cappitelli called his friend, Richard Keyworth, a firefighter and arson investigator for the Elk Grove Village Fire Department. Keyworth had also been monitoring emergency calls. Cappitelli mentioned that the paramedic's report for Mary Kellerman showed that she took Tylenol before she died. Both men were struck by the fact that Tylenol was mentioned in both the Kellerman and Janus reports. "This is a wild stab," Keyworth remarked, "but maybe it's the Tylenol."

Cappitelli's next call was to Chuck Kramer, who confirmed that Adam, Stanley, and Theresa had all taken Tylenol right before collapsing. Cappitelli relayed this information to his supervisor who then called the police to report their suspicions.

An Arlington Heights police officer went to Northwest Community Hospital and informed Dr. Kim that Mary Kellerman had inexplicably died that morning shortly after taking Extra Strength Tylenol. At Dr. Kim's request, the police officer went to the fire station, picked up Kellerman's Tylenol bottle, and brought it to the hospital. Dr. Kim opened the bottle and checked to see if the capsules inside were indeed Tylenol capsules and not some other unknown drug. He put Kellerman's Tylenol bottle in a secure place along with the Janus bottle.

The local emergency workers were beginning to suspect that Mary Kellerman and the Januses had taken poisoned Tylenol capsules, when Paula Prince, a 35-year-old flight attendant, returned to Chicago's O'Hare International Airport late Wednesday evening after a layover out east. On her drive home, she stopped at the Walgreens store on North Wells Street on Chicago's north side and bought a bottle of Extra Strength Tylenol capsules. She then made the short drive to her high-rise apartment on LaSalle Avenue. Once inside her seventh floor apartment, Paula got out of her flight attendant uniform and into a soft robe. She called a friend in her hometown of Omaha, Nebraska, and left a message on her answering machine. Paula then went into the bathroom, swallowed one Extra Strength Tylenol capsule, opened a bottle of cold cream, and began removing her make-up. She collapsed onto the bathroom floor at about 10 p.m.

At Northwest Community Hospital, Dr. Kim was working hard to definitively diagnose the cause of the Januses' deaths. He found a lab in Skokie, Illinois that had a protocol in place for testing cyanide levels in blood samples. Dr. Kim ordered blood samples from Stanley and Theresa to be sent via courier to the Skokie lab. The test results came back at about 1 a.m. They showed lethal levels of cyanide in both blood samples. The cyanide levels were so high that the technician, who had never before conducted such a test, was uncertain of their accuracy.

At about 2 a.m., Dr. Kim called the director of the Skokie lab, Dr. Ambrose, who was at home sleeping, and told him about the high level of cyanide in the Januses' blood samples. Ambrose said he would retest the samples, but he said the technician who ran the initial tests was highly competent, and her results were most certainly accurate. Kim concluded that the Januses had indeed died from cyanide poisoning. For further confirmation, he sent a blood sample from Adam, and a second set of samples from Stanley and Theresa, to the Skokie lab. Dr. Kim also sent the Tylenol bottles from the Janus and Kellerman homes, along with the coffee grounds and peaches from the Janus home, to the Cook County Medical Examiner's Office. He called a staff worker there at about 3 a.m. and asked him to test the Tylenol capsules for cyanide.

*****

The sun had not yet risen on Thursday, September 30, 1982, when Michael Schaffer, the chief toxicologist at the Cook County Medical Examiner's Office, began examining the remaining capsules in the Kellerman and Janus Tylenol bottles. Ten of the capsules were slightly swollen and discolored. Instead of the dry white acetaminophen powder that should have been inside the capsules, they contained a moist, off-white, chunky crystalline substance that he quickly identified as cyanide. These adulterated capsules contained only a trace amount of Tylenol.

"I could smell the cyanide as soon as I opened the containers," Schaffer recalled later. He said the cyanide would have deteriorated the gelatin shell of the capsule rather quickly. As the cyanide-laced capsules appeared to be in the early stages of degradation, officials assumed they must have been filled with cyanide very recently.

When cyanide is moist, a chemical reaction called hydrolysis occurs in which molecules of water are split into hydrogen cations and hydroxyl anions. During the reaction, a small amount of hydrogen cyanide is emitted that smells like bitter almonds. Not everyone can smell this odor, however; the ability to do so is a genetic trait found in about 40 percent of the population. During hydrolysis, polymers like those found in the gelatin-based shells of Tylenol capsules will corrode. The discolored and swollen appearance of ten of the capsules inspected by Schaffer was due to corrosion caused when moisture is transferred from the cyanide to the capsule-shells. The corrosion was not terribly evident, so the victims didn't notice the slightly altered condition of their capsules.

The toxicology tests for Adam, Stanley, and Theresa confirmed that all three had consumed a lethal dose of cyanide. Dr. Kim said the poison had taken effect so quickly that none of them experienced the usual symptoms, such as vomiting, nausea, or dizziness. Later in the morning, Robert Stein confirmed that Mary Kellerman had also died of cyanide poisoning.

Years later, Richard Keyworth reflected on the events of that day: "This (the Tylenol poisonings) could have gone on for years without someone knowing about it. Without talking to each other, the chances of these deaths being connected were slim to none. Who knows how many could have died?"

Keyworth's astute conclusion left a more troubling question unanswered. Had this already gone on for years? The local emergency workers uncovered the Tylenol killer's deadly plot so quickly only because of the sudden deaths of three members of the Janus family on the same day, in the same house, which immediately raised questions.

Theresa Janus's father, Jan Tarasewicz, recognized the importance of the sacrifice that had befallen the Januses and their friends and families. "Our Theresa is gone," he said. "Nothing will bring her back. But all is quiet now. Our people were the victims. They seemed to die for somebody else, so other people could be saved."

The sacrifice of the Januses surely saved others from becoming victims of the Tylenol killer. But could the Tylenol brand be saved? David Collins, the local boy who had done so well after leaving Oak Park, Illinois in 1952, would play a central role in the effort to save Tylenol and the J&J subsidiary that received 100 percent of its revenue from Tylenol products.

4

Guidance of the Credo

In 1982, most of the products Johnson & Johnson was known for—Band-Aids, Adhesive Tapes, Gauze Pads, Cotton Swabs, Johnson & Johnson's Baby Shampoo, Baby Powder, and Baby Oil—were all being manufactured in plants located just outside Chicago. Johnson & Johnson operated more than a dozen facilities in the southwestern part of Chicago. At its height, J&J's 11-plant Bedford Park operation produced 492 products and was a major shipping center for the company. The Johnson & Johnson Consumer Products Company and a J&J subsidiary, Ethicon, were also located in Bedford Park. J&J had a Consumer Products plant and distribution center in nearby Lemont, and a Johnson & Johnson Baby Products plant in Wilmington, Illinois.

The importance of Chicago as a major manufacturing hub for Johnson & Johnson began in 1933 during the depths of the Great Depression. At that time, J&J Chairman Robert Wood Johnson, II, decided to open a manufacturing plant in Chicago to help the company ship its products west faster and more efficiently. Robert Wood Johnson is remembered today for writing *The Credo*, a document that spells out Johnson & Johnson's moral obligation to its employees and to local communities. It puts consumers first, employees second, and shareholders third.

J&J executives said that when they learned about the Tylenol poisonings they simply followed the guidelines in the Credo when determining how to handle the calamity. J&J CEO James Burke said, "The guidance of the Credo played the most important role in the company's decision-making" in the days following the Tylenol murders. "After the crisis was over we realized that no meeting had been called to make the first critical decision. Every one of us knew what we had to do," recalled Burke. "We had the Credo to guide us."

Burke had challenged the relevance of the Credo in the late 1970s because he felt it had become stale. It was "snorted at as an act of pretension," said Burke. So he called a meeting with 35 key executives and suggested they should get rid of the Credo if it didn't mean anything. As he hoped, many were indignant that the Credo might be dismantled and leaped to its defense. "Violent arguments ensued that had the effect of reinvigorating the importance of the Credo," recalled Burke.

Burke said he developed his business philosophy while attending Harvard Business School (HBS), where he received an MBA in 1949. "HBS had a powerful impact on me," said Burke. "When I graduated from college, I was concerned about what I should do with my life. I knew I wanted a career in business, but it wasn't until I was at HBS that I grasped that business could be a force for good in society. We were constantly reminded of the importance of moral values in our decision making. This attention to ethics shaped my entire career."

Burke's career at Johnson & Johnson began in 1953 when he was hired as a product director for the Band-Aid brand. According to a friend and classmate at Harvard, Burke probably skipped years of ladder climbing by making friends when he was a young man with Robert Wood Johnson's son, Bobby Johnson.

After one year with the company, Burke, feeling constrained in his job, briefly interrupted his career at Johnson & Johnson. He quit so he could try his hand at entrepreneurship, launching three separate businesses. He brought out two new products on his own—one was a pink tablet that exploded into bubbles when dropped into a bathtub. Both products bombed, and all three of Burke's business ventures failed.

Less than a year after leaving the company, Burke returned to Johnson & Johnson and took charge of the New Products division. He lured some of the best marketers away from Procter & Gamble, but success still eluded him. Burke later described how his boss had taken him to task early in his career, saying, "You're a bachelor, and you're bright. I'll accept that you can bring a lot to the business. I'll even accept that maybe Bobby Johnson is right about you; that you can someday run this company. But I don't see that in you. And I don't see any indication that you want to pay the price to do it. Now, if you do, we'll take it a step at a time. You have this job for a year, and this door is open. Whenever you want me I'm available."

Reflecting back on that conversation, Burke admitted, "He really gave it to me, and he was right."

With a growing list of disappointing new product launches, Robert Wood Johnson soon summoned Burke into his office. Burke thought he was in trouble for his latest failure, a combination nose drops and spray for children, aptly called Johnson & Johnson's Nose Drops and Spray.

At the scheduled time, Burke entered Johnson's office, expecting the worst. "I thought I was going to get fired," he said later.

Johnson, who was seated behind his desk, tossed out a bottle of Johnson & Johnson's Nose Drops and Spray. "Are you the man who launched this thing?" asked Johnson.

Burke nervously replied that he was.

Johnson stood up and grasped Burke's hand. "I want to congratulate you," said Johnson. "Business is about taking risk. Keep doing it. Don't ever make these mistakes again," he warned, "but please make many other mistakes. That's what we're paying you for."

Burke moved up in the company, initially focusing on marketing and advertising. In 1961, Johnson & Johnson formed a new division called the Robert Wood Johnson Company. Burke was put in charge of this new division, which handled the marketing of Johnson & Johnson's baby products and many of its proprietary products, including Tylenol.

Johnson & Johnson acquired Tylenol through its purchase of McNeil Laboratories in 1959. McNeil had first marketed prescription drugs containing acetaminophen, the active ingredient in Tylenol, in 1953. J&J launched Tylenol as an over-the-counter (OTC) medication in 1960, but continued to market Tylenol primarily to hospitals where it was used extensively. In 1961, J&J

moved the McNeil Laboratories headquarters from Philadelphia to a newly constructed facility in Fort Washington, Pennsylvania.

In 1975, when Burke was President of Johnson & Johnson, he got his chance to take Tylenol into the mass market with the full backing of Johnson & Johnson's vast resources. Bristol Myers had just introduced Datril with a series of advertisements promoting it as being much less expensive than Tylenol while having the same ingredients. Burke convinced J&J's Chairman, Richard Sellars, that they should meet the new competition head-on. Burke began aggressively marketing Tylenol directly to consumers. His efforts to grow the Tylenol business paid off almost immediately, and in 1976 he was appointed CEO of Johnson & Johnson and chairman of the company's Board of Directors.

In 1978, McNeil Laboratories became McNeilab Inc., and J&J formed two new operating companies under the McNeilab umbrella: the McNeil Pharmaceutical Company and the McNeil Consumer Products Company. James Burke and Wayne Nelson, who was the first chairman of the reorganized McNeil, formed the McNeil Consumer Products Company to sell only non-prescription products that contained acetaminophen. At the time, those products were Tylenol, CoTylenol, Children's Tylenol products, and Sine-Aid. A large annual Tylenol advertising budget, which grew to $85 million by 1982, helped the company increase its share of the OTC pain-reliever market from 4 percent in 1976 to 37 percent in 1982.

5

What Happened in Chicago?

Dr. Edmund Donoghue, the deputy assistant medical examiner for Cook County, Illinois, held a press conference at around 8 a.m. (Central time) Thursday morning, September 30, 1982 to report the deaths of the Janus brothers in Arlington Heights and Mary Kellerman in neighboring Elk Grove Village. Donoghue said they had died on Wednesday from cardio-pulmonary collapse after taking Extra Strength Tylenol capsules. He said the investigation had definitely confirmed the presence of cyanide in the Tylenol capsules.

Theresa Janus, who was being kept alive on life support machines, would be declared dead on Friday. Officials had not yet linked the deaths of Lynn Reiner and Mary McFarland to cyanide-laced Tylenol. The body of Paula Prince would not be discovered until Friday evening.

Just prior to Donoghue's press conference in Chicago, Jim Ritter, a *Chicago Sun-Times* reporter, had called a J&J public relations executive James Murray at Johnson & Johnson's headquarters in New Brunswick, New Jersey. Ritter was seeking information about the history and sales volume of Tylenol. Murray, sensing something was wrong, ended his call with Ritter and dialed McNeil's Public Relations Director Elsie Behmer.

"Is this about the terrible thing that happened in Chicago?" Behmer asked.

"No. What happened in Chicago?" Murray replied.

"We heard some people have been poisoned with Tylenol capsules," said Behmer. "I'm going down to a meeting right now to find out more."

As soon as Murray put the phone back on the hook, another call came in. It was Ritter again. He had just found out why he had been asked a few minutes earlier to obtain the background information on Tylenol, and now he wanted a comment from Murray on the Tylenol poisonings.

He didn't get one.

Murray's next call went to Arthur Quilty, a member of the J&J Executive Committee. Quilty had worked his way up through the ranks of Johnson & Johnson's Personal Products Company and was now the company group chairman of Johnson & Johnson Products, Inc., a group of companies that included the McNeil Consumer Products Company.

When the call came in from Murray, Quilty's first reaction was disbelief. "Are you sure this isn't a hoax?" he asked. It didn't take long for him to be convinced that it wasn't.

Down the hall from Quilty's fifth-floor executive office, J&J President David Clare was meeting with James Burke. In the vernacular of Johnson & Johnson, it was their regular bimonthly "one-on-one" meeting. Burke and Clare were engaged in a casual conversation regarding the company's healthcare program when Quilty barged in and told them about the poisonings just outside Chicago. Burke immediately picked up the phone and called David Collins, whose office was located several floors below.

Earlier that month, Collins had been appointed company group chairman, chairman of the McNeil Consumer Products Company, and a member of Johnson & Johnson's twelve-man executive committee. Collins's promotion had been so sudden and recent that the J&J facilities management group had not yet moved his office up to the fifth floor where the offices of all the executive committee members were located.

Collins had received a B.A. degree from the University of Notre Dame in 1956, and a L.L.B. from Harvard Law School in 1959. He was a former general counsel for Johnson & Johnson, and had followed an unusual career path that took him from the company's legal department to several top executive positions at J&J operating companies. Of his recent promotion, Collins said, "It was a felicitous appointment for me, or so I thought at the time. Before this promotion, I had responsibility for Mexico, where there had been two devaluations in one year, Central America where there had been a war, and several South American countries experiencing rampant inflation and more devaluations. I was coming from a scenario of problems to McNeil, a company with a great future and what I thought was an opportunity to win a few."

Collins was on the phone with an executive at a J&J subsidiary in Mexico when his secretary cut in to say that Burke was on the other line and it was an emergency. Collins told her to relay the message that he would head up to Burke's office as soon as he finished handling his own emergency. The Mexican government had implemented new monetary controls to try to curb the plunging value of the peso. If Collins could not get supplies fast enough to his Mexican company, it would be out of business by the end of the year. Collins soon finished his conversation with the executive in Mexico and made his way up to Burke's office, where Quilty, Clare, Burke, and McNeil President Joseph Chiesa had already begun to plan their strategy on how to handle the looming crisis.

Larry Foster, J&J's vice president of public relations, had taken the day off and was at home writing a book titled *A Company That Cares, the History of Johnson & Johnson*. Foster had been a reporter, bureau chief, and night editor of New Jersey's largest newspaper, *The Newark News*, before Robert Wood Johnson, II, hired him in 1957 to help form Johnson & Johnson's first public relations department.

Sometime around mid-morning Foster received a call from James Murray with news of the Tylenol problem. "That was a bombshell," Foster said later. Foster made a beeline to New Brunswick, arriving at Johnson & Johnson headquarters 45 minutes after he'd received Murray's call. He rushed to Burke's office and joined the strategy session.

"I never came home for two days," said Foster. "Slept in the office—what sleep we had."

"One-word description of my reaction—disbelief…Second description—two words—total disbelief," remarked Foster. "I think that this best described how many in the company felt that our product could have been used as a murder weapon. I mean, a product that is designed to help you take care of pain would be used as a murder weapon?"

Tylenol was bringing in $450 million in annual revenue, and the brand accounted for 15 to 20 percent of Johnson & Johnson's profits. No other J&J product generated anywhere near the revenue and profit of Tylenol. Following the Thursday morning news conference in Chicago, announcing the deaths from poisoned Tylenol, J&J executives acted quickly to protect that revenue stream.

Burke immediately focused his efforts on getting the right men in place at the scene of the crime and at J&J and McNeil headquarters. He named six senior executives to an Emergency Strategy Group. The group included J&J President David Clare, International Company Group Chairman Wayne Nelson, Company Group Chairman Arthur Quilty, Company Group Chairman David Collins, Corporate Public Relations Vice President Lawrence "Larry" Foster, and J&J General Counsel George Frazza. The group met at 9 a.m. and 5 p.m. every day for close to six weeks to make decisions on how the evolving Tylenol situation should be handled. Many times, according to Foster, the morning meeting was still in session when the evening meeting was scheduled to begin.

Burke initially hoped the news media would identify Tylenol only as a McNeil product. With this objective in mind, Burke told David Collins to take a lawyer, a public relations aide, and a security expert and fly out to McNeil headquarters in Fort Washington to manage the crisis and handle the media from there. Burke commanded Collins to "Take charge."

Meanwhile, police cruisers in Arlington Heights and Elk Grove Village roamed the streets with loudspeakers blaring warnings of unexplained deaths possibly attributed to Tylenol. Jewel Companies, Inc., the Chicago-based owner of Jewel Food, Osco Drug, and Jewel-Osco stores, ordered all their stores to pull Extra Strength Tylenol capsules from the shelves Thursday morning. Walgreens, also based in Chicago, ordered its stores in the Midwest to remove Tylenol from their shelves at 9:15 a.m. and expanded the order nationwide at 11:15 a.m. Most retailers outside the Chicago area stopped selling only the Tylenol from Lot MC2880, which was the lot number on both the Janus and Kellerman Tylenol bottles, the only ones known to contain cyanide at the time.

Authorities soon traced the Tylenol in the Kellerman and the Janus bottles, which had been purchased from two separate Jewel stores, to a warehouse in the Chicago suburb of Franklin Park. But they never identified the owner of that warehouse. The Tylenol had been manufactured at McNeil's Fort Washington plant in April 1982 and distributed to states east of the Mississippi River and to North Dakota, South Dakota, Nebraska, and Eastern Wyoming.

Initially, Johnson & Johnson did not recall any Tylenol capsules. Instead, the company faxed mailgrams to retailers and wholesalers, assuring them that the problem rested in Chicago and was limited to Extra Strength Tylenol capsules from Lot MC2880. By noon Thursday, J&J had faxed about 450 thousand of these mailgrams to physicians, hospitals, and wholesalers. The mailgram read in part, "We currently have no evidence that any other Extra Strength Tylenol capsule product or any other Tylenol product was similarly contaminated."

6

J&J Takes Charge

Ninety minutes after James Burke had told David Collins to take charge of the Tylenol problem, the corporate helicopter carrying Collins and several other J&J executives touched down at McNeil headquarters in Fort Washington, 60 miles west of Johnson & Johnson's corporate office. Once inside the building, Collins picked up the phone and called attorney Paul Noland, a childhood friend and college roommate from his days at Notre Dame University. Noland was a partner in the law firm of Rooks, Pitts, and Poust, with offices in Chicago and Wheaton, Illinois. He had previously handled product liability cases in the Chicago area for Johnson & Johnson.

Collins asked Noland to go down to the Cook County Medical Examiner's Office, find out as much as he could, and then call him back at McNeil. "I needed my own eyes and ears on the scene," Collins said later.

Collins also called another attorney pal, Francis "Mike" Heroux, and asked him to help J&J manage the crisis. Heroux, like Noland, was a partner at Rooks, Pitts, and Poust, in the firm's Wheaton office in DuPage County. Heroux, Noland, and Collins had all graduated in 1952 from Fenwick High School, a private Catholic prep-school in Oak Park, Illinois.

Collins was later inducted into the Fenwick High School Hall of Fame. When addressing the Fenwick students and alumni attending his induction ceremony, Collins called Fenwick "a place to build strong friendships that can help you through many situations and a place to think about the values you will take with you through life." In the fall of 1982, with the Tylenol brand in big trouble, Collins needed all the help he could get from his many friends still living near his Oak Park alma mater.

Illinois Governor Jim Thompson, who also grew up in Oak Park, said the mad Tylenol killer was "putting a state, indeed a nation, into fear." Thompson, the governor of Illinois since 1977, had been the U.S. attorney in the Northern District of Illinois in the early 1970s. He had graduated from Northwestern Law School in 1959, along with Mike Heroux, who was now a member of J&J's outside counsel handling the Tylenol murders crisis.

Governor Thompson put Illinois Attorney General Tyrone Fahner in charge of the investigative team dubbed the Tylenol task force, which quickly grew to 140 local, state, and federal investigators. Thompson had appointed Fahner to the job of top Illinois lawyer-lawman in July 1980 when the immensely popular, long-time Attorney General, William Scott, was convicted of tax evasion and sentenced to 11 months in prison. Having never run for office, Fahner was a political neophyte. He was a virtual unknown, even to the residents of his home state. But that anonymity changed instantly when he became the official spokesperson for the task force charged with solving the Tylenol murders.

Fahner was currently in the midst of a seemingly hopeless campaign to be elected Attorney General for a full 4-year term. A *Chicago Tribune* Poll released on October 2, 1982, one month before Election Day, showed Fahner trailing former Lieutenant Governor Neil Hartigan by 20 percentage points. However, after Fahner became the official spokesperson of the Tylenol task force, he was seen on television every day and his standing in the polls steadily improved.

One of Fahner's first official acts as the head of the Tylenol task force was to advise Illinois residents to gather up all their Tylenol capsules and flush them down the toilet. Chicago police officers were also counseled to tell Chicago area residents to destroy all their Tylenol products. NBC's Chicago affiliate, WMAQ-TV, aired a video clip of a Chicago police dispatcher announcing over the police radio on Thursday September 30th that Tylenol products "may be contaminated with cyanide, and should be destroyed." Some of the destroyed capsules surely contained cyanide and could have helped investigators track down the Tylenol killer.

*****

After David Collins got his lawyers in place in Illinois on Thursday morning, he turned his attention to the hectic situation at McNeil headquarters. Thirty-three telephones were set up to handle the incoming calls. Larry Foster said there were about 150 to 175 calls the first day, and over the course of the weeks ahead, something like 2,500 reporters covered the story. His staff kept a log of every reporter's name and the response they were given. Foster sensed early on that the reporters from the television, print, and radio media thought Johnson & Johnson was a victim and would, therefore, be cast publicly as a victim.

Regarding the possibility that the cyanide had been put into the Tylenol at the manufacturing plant, McNeil Communications Director, Elsie Behmer, proclaimed, "We were clean." Behmer said some of the bulk Tylenol powder from the recalled MC2880 batch still at the plant had been tested, and it was uncontaminated. She said the company did not work with cyanide, and Tylenol was the only product produced at the plant. Much of that work was done by machine said Behmer, thus lessening the possibility of employee sabotage.

Larry Foster also assured reporters that cyanide was not stored at the Tylenol manufacturing plant or used in the production of Tylenol. One day later, however, J&J was forced to retract that statement. Foster admitted that cyanide was in fact stored and used at the McNeil manufacturing plants. McNeil used cyanide on a daily basis to test Povidone, the primary binder used in making Tylenol.

McNeil President Joseph Chiesa received continuous updates from harried managers as new reports came in of fatalities and other supposed poisonings, the vast majority of which were not actually Tylenol poisonings. McNeil executives used a felt-tip marker to write down each bit of information on drawing paper attached to a big easel. As the reports accumulated, the sheets were ripped from the easel and pinned on the walls in a large conference room. Soon the walls were covered with dozens of sheets of paper, each containing disparate bits of information with arrows drawn between them: victims, causes of deaths, lot numbers on the poisoned Tylenol bottles, the outlets where they'd been purchased, dates when they'd been manufactured, and the route they'd taken through the distribution system. The data on those sheets of paper were never revealed to the public.

A two-way video conference link was established between J&J headquarters in New Brunswick and McNeil headquarters in Fort Washington to facilitate face-to-face meetings between the executives at the two sites. Twenty-five public relations employees from other J&J operating companies were recruited to assist the public relations staff of fifteen at J&J headquarters. Public relations personnel from both McNeil and J&J coordinated a media response to minimize any suspicion that the company was at fault.

Foster said the public relations department had complete support from management to immediately make the first important decision that pointed Johnson & Johnson's public relations program in the right direction. That decision, said Foster, was for the company to cooperate fully with all types of news media.

In reality, Johnson & Johnson kept reporters at bay throughout the entire crisis. Only a few J&J employees talked to the press, typically on a one-on-one basis over the telephone. After releasing a few brief public statements in the first two days of the investigation, the public relations department went into lockdown mode and followed a policy of silence regarding any new information relevant to the Tylenol tamperings. J&J never held a press conference about the Tylenol poisonings or took questions in an open forum. James Burke did make appearances on *60 Minutes* and the *Donahue Show*, but he made those appearances more than four weeks after the murders for the sole purpose of promoting Tylenol in its new tamper-resistant packaging.

Foster took care of the media for Johnson & Johnson, while J&J Public Relations Director Robert Kniffin went to Fort Washington to handle the calls that came in to McNeil headquarters. Robert Andrews, the assistant director of public relations for J&J, was put in charge of handling the media in Chicago.

Andrews, along with security, public relations personnel, and 30 toxicologists, were dispatched by corporate jet to Chicago to work with the authorities there and to establish J&J's own lab. Upon their arrival at O'Hare International Airport, Andrews and two other J&J executives drove to Elk Grove Village and met with detectives and evidence technicians for an hour-and-a-half Thursday afternoon, September 30th. Andrews told reporters in Chicago that his firm was "collectively shocked." He said Johnson & Johnson had launched an investigation that morning to track down the Tylenol capsules from Lot MC2880.

7

The Hospital

The autopsy of Lynn Reiner had just begun at 9:45 a.m. on Thursday morning, September 30th, when the DuPage County Coroner's Office received a call from Captain Enders of the Winfield Fire Department. Enders, who had been involved in the rescue call for Lynn the previous day, told Deputy Coroner Peter Siekmann that Lynn had taken Tylenol shortly before she collapsed. Enders also advised Siekmann about the news reports of the Tylenol poisonings in Arlington Heights and Elk Grove Village.

Siekmann called Winfield Police Chief Carl Sostak and asked him to go out to Reiner's home to "retrieve any and all bottles of Tylenol or any Tylenol capsules which may not have been in any bottle." This statement, which Siekmann documented in the coroner's report, implied that Siekmann had prior knowledge or at least a hunch that Reiner's cyanide-laced Extra Strength Tylenol capsules had been dispensed in a unit-dose package at the hospital, and thus would not have been in a bottle.

Late Thursday morning, Winfield Police Officer Scott Watkins, accompanied by Chief Sostak, returned to the Reiner home to investigate what they now suspected was a murder. Sostak and Watkins searched Reiner's home for Tylenol capsules, Tylenol bottles, and any other potential evidence. They found one bottle of Regular Strength Tylenol sitting on a shelf above the kitchen sink. Printed on the bottle's label was the lot number, 1833MB. Police also found the box for the Regular Strength Tylenol bottle.

Watkins and Sostak sat down with Ed Reiner and gently questioned him about the events leading up to his wife's death. Ed said that he had left the house before 3 p.m. Wednesday afternoon to pick up his daughters, Michelle and Dawn, from school. He had dropped Dawn off at a friend's house before returning home with Michelle at about 3:30 p.m.

Chief Sostak asked Ed what he knew about his wife's trip to the Frank's Finer Foods store where she purchased the bottle of Regular Strength Tylenol.

Ed said that just before he left to pick up his daughters, Lynn had mentioned that she had a headache and was going to run out to the store to pick up some Tylenol.

Sostak asked Ed if he knew how the Extra Strength Tylenol capsules had gotten into Lynn's bottle of Regular Strength Tylenol.

Ed said he didn't know. He figured that they must have been in the bottle when Lynn bought it.

After Sostak and Watkins finished questioning Ed, Sostak brought the Tylenol capsules and Tylenol packages recovered from Reiner's home to the DuPage County Coroner's Office in Wheaton. Peter Siekmann then brought the capsules to the Illinois Department of Health lab, also in Wheaton, just before 5 p.m. that evening. Toxicologists completed tests on these capsules shortly after midnight. Joerg Pirl, the assistant chief toxicologist for the Illinois Department of Public Health, said the cyanide in the capsules was potassium cyanide. He said that this particular potassium cyanide was a technical grade, an inexpensive, low-purity grade typically used in heavy industry, as opposed to the more expensive high-purity grade used in laboratories.

Siekmann told reporters that shortly before Lynn Reiner died, she had taken two Extra Strength Tylenol capsules, one that contained cyanide, from a bottle containing other capsules laced with cyanide. He said four of the remaining six Extra Strength Tylenol capsules had been filled completely with cyanide. None of Lynn's Regular Strength Tylenol capsules contained cyanide.

Siekmann said the lot number for Lynn's Extra Strength capsules was not immediately known because she had carried them in a bottle of Regular Strength Tylenol capsules. However, the likely source of Lynn's Extra Strength capsules was the hospital.

Moms like Lynn Reiner were routinely given Tylenol at hospital maternity wards. In fact, 90 percent of all non-prescription pain pills given to hospital patients in 1982 were Tylenol pills. So it makes perfect sense that before Lynn checked out of the hospital on Tuesday, September 28th, she was given a package of eight Extra Strength Tylenol capsules.

Central DuPage Hospital had converted its pharmacy to a unit-dose system in 1974. Unit-dose pharmacies received drugs in bulk containers, typically holding 100 to 1,000 pills, and then dispensed the pills in appropriate amounts to inpatients and outpatients. Drugs dispensed at unit-dose pharmacies in 1982 were typically packaged at the pharmacy in blister packs or plastic pouches in amounts ranging from one dose to one day's worth of doses.

The American Society of Hospital Pharmacists (ASHP) published guidelines in 1980 for hospital-pharmacies, stating that for most medications, not more than a 24-hour supply of doses should be provided to outpatients at any one time (patients checking out of the hospital are considered outpatients). At the then recommended dose of two capsules every six hours, Lynn's eight Extra Strength Tylenol capsules represented exactly a 24-hour supply.

The cyanide-laced Tylenol capsule that killed Lynn Reiner must have come from a unit-dose package dispensed at the closed-door pharmacy in Central DuPage Hospital. That pharmacy was inaccessible to the public, and thus it was inaccessible to the alleged madman who had supposedly put cyanide-laced capsules into Tylenol bottles that had been sitting on the shelves of Chicago-area retail stores.

The ASHP guidelines contained additional recommendations also relevant to the Reiner case:

> Inpatient self-care and "discharge" medications are to be labeled as outpatient prescriptions. Outpatient medications are to be labeled in accordance with State Board of Pharmacy and federal regulations. Medications given to patients as "discharge medication" are to be labeled in the pharmacy (not by the nursing personnel) as outpatient prescriptions. The source of the medication and the initials of the dispenser are to be noted on the prescription form at the time of dispensing. If feasible, the lot number also is recorded. Nonprescription drugs are labeled like any other medication.

One day after the poisonings, the Tylenol capsules in the pharmacy at Central DuPage Hospital were quarantined in accordance with ASHP guidelines, which stated that in the event of a recall, the hospital pharmacists are to "quarantine all recalled products they obtained (marked "Quarantined—Do Not Use") until they are picked up by or returned to the manufacturer." By Thursday afternoon, September 30th, J&J had assigned Chicago-area sales reps the job of checking to make sure local retailers and hospitals were not selling Extra Strength Tylenol capsules. J&J later removed and destroyed the Tylenol capsules from Central DuPage Hospital and other Chicago area outlets. The capsules from those outlets were never inspected.

*****

Late Thursday morning, the pathologist who had conducted the autopsy of Mary McFarland's body revealed that the examination for CVA (Cerebral Vascular Accident, i.e., stroke) was inconclusive. The Lombard police then began to look into the possibility that her death had been caused by cyanide-laced Tylenol. A detective called Mary's father and asked him to check her belongings for analgesic capsules. When he looked through his daughter's purse, he found a small Dristan bottle. The bottle held ten Extra Strength Tylenol capsules—five contained cyanide.

Lombard police went to Mary's home on Thursday afternoon and found an empty Extra Strength Tylenol bottle bearing lot number MB2738 in the bathroom trash can. They also found a bottle of Extra Strength Tylenol capsules marked with the lot number 1910MD in the medicine cabinet. Of the remaining 33 Tylenol capsules in that 50-count bottle, one contained cyanide. Police determined that the cyanide-laced Tylenol capsules in Mary's Dristan bottle had also come from the Tylenol bottle marked with lot number 1910MD.

Lombard police detectives visited all the retail stores surrounding Mary's home and work to check for other bottles of Extra Strength Tylenol capsules from Lot 1910MD. Only the Woolworth store in the mall where Mary worked carried Tylenol from that lot. The coroner's inquest report confirmed that Mary had purchased the cyanide-laced Tylenol at the Woolworth store. This conclusion was further confirmed in a lawsuit filed by the Tylenol victims' families, naming Woolworth as a defendant and the source of Mary's bottle of cyanide-laced Tylenol.

The deaths of Mary McFarland and Lynn Reiner had not yet been connected to cyanide-laced Tylenol when James Burke decided on Thursday afternoon to recall all Tylenol capsules from Lot MC2880. J&J said the recall consisted of 93,000 fifty-count bottles of Extra Strength Tylenol capsules.

J&J spokesperson Robert Kniffin said the Tylenol batch from Lot MC2880 had gone directly from a McNeil Consumer Products Company plant in Fort Washington to a warehouse sometime between the 19th and 25th of August 1982. However, the Tylenol did not go directly from McNeil to a warehouse in Illinois. It first went through a warehouse in Montgomeryville, Pennsylvania—one of eleven regional distribution centers owned and operated by Johnson & Johnson. These J&J distribution centers were not mentioned in 1982 by J&J executives, but they were referenced in a 1983 Harvard Business School case study about the dynamics involved in Johnson & Johnson's decision in September 1982 to centralize its order fulfillment and sales and logistics operations.

Three years later, Robert Kniffin revealed that Tylenol was distributed through three J&J regional distribution centers located in Montgomeryville, Pennsylvania; Round Rock, Texas; and Glendale, California. J&J shipped Tylenol through these same regional distribution centers in 1982—a fact confirmed by several Department of Defense (DOD) contracts retrieved from the National Archives database. In the 1970s and 1980s, the DOD contracted with McNeil to buy Tylenol products from the J&J facilities in Round Rock, Glendale, Montgomeryville, and Fort Washington. Kniffin said the Montgomeryville distribution center shipped Tylenol to warehouses located primarily east of the Mississippi River.

*****

News of what became known as the 'Tylenol crisis' was broadcast Thursday evening on all three networks. The Tylenol murders case, given the code-name TYMURS (an abbreviation of TYlenol MURderS) by the FBI, was the most extensively covered news event since the assassination of John F. Kennedy. Over 100,000 separate articles about the poisonings ran in U.S. newspapers. National and local television news programs broadcast hundreds of hours of coverage. Poison control centers nationwide reported being swamped with calls from worried consumers who had taken Tylenol capsules. One Chicago hospital received 700 calls about Tylenol in one day.

Overnight, the market share for Tylenol dropped from 37 percent of the over-the-counter (OTC) analgesic market to just 7 percent. Many public relations experts predicted the end of the Tylenol brand. "I don't think they can ever sell another product under that name," said Jerry Della Femina, a well-known and outspoken advertising executive. "There may be an advertising person who thinks he can solve this and if they find him, I want to hire him, because then I want him to turn our water cooler into a wine cooler."

8

The Expanding Tylenol Problem

After a long day at McNeil headquarters on Thursday, September 30th, David Collins checked into a nearby hotel shortly after midnight. He went to bed at about 2 a.m. only to be awakened one hour later when the bedside telephone rang. Collins later said that the caller had informed him that the lot number on Mary McFarland's bottle of adulterated Tylenol indicated it had come from McNeil's Tylenol manufacturing plant in Round Rock, Texas. The Tylenol in McFarland's bottle was from Lot 1910MD and had been manufactured in May 1982 and distributed in August to warehouses in the Chicago area and in states west of the Mississippi River.

As the cyanide-laced Tylenol had come from two different lots, manufactured in two separate facilities, officials said they were confident that none of the poisoned Tylenol capsules had been adulterated at either of the McNeil plants. A coordinated effort by multiple employees to poison Tylenol capsules at two separate plants was improbable, giving some support to Burke's decision to not recall all Tylenol capsules nationwide. Yet the fact that the adulterated Tylenol had been manufactured in two different plants was, according to David Collins, exactly what led J&J to expand the Tylenol recall to include all 171,000 bottles of Extra Strength Tylenol capsules from Lot 1910MD.

"The fact that the second batch came from Round Rock didn't say a damn thing to me," Collins recalled later, "Except that, oh Jesus, now I've got two lots to recall instead of one."

In truth, J&J did not intend to recall Tylenol from lot 1910MD—at least not initially. A McNeil spokesperson told reporters on Friday morning, October 1st that the company "wouldn't make a decision on extending the voluntary withdrawal of its product to additional lot numbers until there was more definitive information about the capsules consumed by [Mary McFarland]." Larry Foster and J&J spokesperson Marshall Malloy both confirmed that the company was not issuing a recall for the Tylenol batch labeled Lot 1910MD. However, while J&J executives were reassuring the public that a recall of Tylenol from Lot 1910MD was unnecessary, McNeil representatives were rushing out to the Value Drug warehouse in Altoona, Pennsylvania to inspect Extra Strength Tylenol capsules from that very lot.

Jeff Montgomery, a reporter for the *Altoona Mirror*, had interviewed the owner of Value Drug that Friday. The owner told Montgomery that during a one-hour period that morning, he had three conversations with three different McNeil representatives regarding the Tylenol in his warehouse. "They checked us three times within an hour this morning," he said. "Naturally, we heard it all on television late last night, and the first thing this morning, McNeil was on the phone giving us the two lot numbers to check. At 8:30 a.m. a McNeil pharmaceutical salesman checked our stock, and at 9 a.m. a McNeil consumer products man from Pittsburgh came and checked it again."

"I think they bent over backwards," said the Value Drug owner, referring to the intense, rapid communication from McNeil officials and the speed with which they checked his stock of Tylenol capsules.

Larry Foster said the fact that the cyanide-laced Tylenol came from two sources, but cropped up in only one area, "leads us to believe strongly that the problem rests in Chicago." But the urgent visits by McNeil executives to the Value Drug warehouse, located 563 miles east of the Tylenol murders crime scene, indicated that J&J executives suspected that the Tylenol problem was not limited to just the Chicago area. Foster and J&J President David Clare later said that J&J executives were worried that the poisoned Tylenol capsules may have been a nationwide problem.

Two decades after the Tylenol murders, when Foster was in a forum where he could calmly reflect back on that time, he recalled the concern of J&J executives who feared that the poisoned Tylenol capsules were not restricted to the Chicago area. "We naturally wanted to protect the good name of J&J and McNeil," said Foster, "and we wanted to get the product off the market for fear that it might be a nationwide plot."

Though Collins said he didn't know until 3 a.m. Friday morning that the Tylenol from Lot 1910MD had been manufactured at the Round Rock plant—he actually must have known all along where it had been manufactured. That information was incorporated into the lot number, as required by the U.S. Code of Federal Regulations, Title 21, Section 201.18, which states: "The lot number on the label of a drug should be capable of yielding the complete manufacturing history of the package. An incorrect lot number may be regarded as causing the article to be misbranded."

The alpha characters in the lot numbers for the Tylenol manufactured in Round Rock came after the numeric characters (i.e., 1910MD), whereas the alpha characters for the lots manufactured in Fort Washington came before the numeric characters (i.e., MC2880). It was the first numeric digit of each lot code that actually identified the manufacturing plant. The first numeric digit of the lot codes for Tylenol manufactured at Fort Washington was "2", and for Round Rock it was "1".

The 3 a.m. Friday morning phone call to David Collins had not been made because someone had suddenly figured out that the Tylenol from Lot 1910MD had been manufactured in Round Rock. That phone call may have been made because someone at Johnson & Johnson had uncovered an urgent problem regarding the distribution of potentially poisoned Tylenol to warehouses outside the Chicago area.

Late Thursday morning, soon after the McNeil officials visited the Value Drug warehouse, J&J executives reversed their earlier decision and recalled all Tylenol capsules from Lot 1910MD. J&J had now recalled 264,000 bottles of Extra Strength Tylenol capsules from two lots, representing 2.4 percent of the 11 million bottles in the distribution system, retail stores, and hospitals.

The public was just learning about this second recall when Chicago police detectives were called to Paula Prince's north side apartment Friday evening at around 5 p.m. Paula had died

Wednesday night, September 29th, but she had the following day off and wasn't missed until she failed to show up for work on Friday afternoon. Her sister became concerned and drove to Paula's apartment to check on her. She unlocked the door with her spare key and then entered the apartment where she found Paula's body lying on the bathroom floor. A bottle of Extra Strength Tylenol capsules was sitting on the vanity. One capsule from the 24-count bottle was missing.

The detectives took possession of Paula's Tylenol bottle and then searched the apartment until they found the receipt showing that Paula had purchased the Tylenol at the nearby Walgreens store. Later, while viewing video footage from a security camera mounted above the automatic teller machine in that Walgreens store, police found a photo of Paula Prince paying for her bottle of Extra Strength Tylenol. The camera had automatically snapped the picture at about 9 p.m. Wednesday night when someone withdrew cash from the teller machine.

Chicago Police Superintendant Richard Brzeczek said one of the remaining twenty-three capsules in Prince's bottle contained cyanide, but six others were slightly discolored. The moisture from the two cyanide-laced capsules had leached onto six of the surrounding capsules, causing them to corrode slightly. The Tylenol in Prince's bottle was from Lot 1801MA and had been manufactured at the McNeil plant in Round Rock, Texas. This Tylenol, like the Tylenol involved in all the other poisonings, had been shipped to a warehouse in Illinois from Johnson & Johnson's regional distribution center in Montgomeryville, Pennsylvania.

Chicago Mayor Jane Byrne held a news conference late Friday night that went well past midnight. Byrne asked all city residents to turn in their Tylenol to local police stations, along with a note detailing where and when it was purchased. "Don't take Tylenol," she warned, "not even tablet or liquid form."

The FDA had released a far less expansive alert several hours earlier, advising consumers to stop using only Extra Strength Tylenol capsules. The FDA had also already announced that Johnson & Johnson bore no responsibility for the tamperings. This exoneration seemed premature, because at this point, just two days into the investigation, the FDA could not have conducted even a preliminary investigation of the Tylenol manufacturing plants. Standard FDA inspections of manufacturing plants take place over a period of days, often lasting several weeks.

The FDA was surprisingly ill-equipped in 1982 to make any determination regarding the security of the Tylenol manufacturing and distribution network. In a report to the U.S. Congress on April 26, 1982, the U.S. Government Accountability Office (GAO) concluded that the FDA was unable to evaluate the relative magnitude of any identified problem with an OTC product. The GAO report said the FDA is unaware of the number of individual OTC products currently being marketed and whether these products are safe and effective as determined by any type of FDA review.

Incredibly, up until 1997, the FDA had no statutory authority to inspect records or documents at OTC drug manufacturing plants. After a 1991 investigation of the FDA's procedures for monitoring OTC drugs, the GAO determined that the lack of full access to OTC drug manufacturers' records and files limited the FDA's ability to evaluate the effectiveness of these manufacturers' efforts to analyze complaints, remedy problems, and generally produce a safe and effective product.

The FDA, because it did not have access to records or documents at the McNeil manufacturing plants, did not even know about the nearly 300 consumer complaints of Tylenol tamperings, mix-ups, and contaminations that Johnson & Johnson had received in the three years prior to the Tylenol murders. The existence of these complaints was not disclosed until 1991 when Johnson & Johnson was forced to turn them over to the lawyers handling the lawsuits filed by the relatives of the Tylenol murders victims. In describing these complaints, Bruce Pfaff, an attorney for some of the plaintiffs, said, "Either capsules were missing, or some other medication was mixed in or there were foreign objects, pieces of metal, and even fingernails."

9

Rational Evildoer

According to the stories widely reported in the news-media, the Tylenol killer had put the cyanide-laced Tylenol capsules into the Tylenol bottles *after* the bottles were delivered to Chicago-area retail stores. J&J executives and FDA officials suggested, but never stated outright, that the tamperings occurred in the retail stores. In fact, there was no evidence to support this hypothesis. Larry Foster, on the day he learned about the Tylenol poisonings, admitted that the tamperings may have occurred in the distribution channel. "We believe [the tamperings] happened somewhere in the distribution or at the point of sale," said Foster.

Jim Adamson, a spokesperson for the FDA's regional office in Kansas City, Missouri, said authorities believed that the recalled bottles were tampered with during the distribution process.

Tyrone Fahner initially indicated that the employees in the distribution channel were potential suspects. On Friday, October 1st, he said that authorities were seeking lists of all employees of retailers and all people in the distribution chain who could have handled the tainted Tylenol. "We're investigating stereotypes of disgruntled employees…all along the production chain," Fahner remarked. He said investigators had already identified 20 to 30 potential suspects and had begun combing the personnel files of people who might have had access to the Tylenol.

In the following days, however, Fahner embraced the story of a Tylenol killer who had put the poisoned capsules into Tylenol bottles that had been sitting on the shelves of Chicago area retail stores. Fahner also laid out the basic premise of this tampering-in-the-retail-stores theory—the "approved theory" for the Tylenol murders. He said the Tylenol was not tampered with until it reached the stores, ruling out the possibility that the capsules were filled with cyanide during either manufacturing or distribution. Fahner said the cyanide-spiked capsules probably were placed in the stores on Tuesday, September 28th, apparently at the front of the shelves to ensure that they would sell quickly. He said the killer began with one bottle of cyanide-laced Tylenol capsules and went from store to store replacing a random number of Tylenol capsules in bottles already in the stores, with poisoned capsules.

Fahner claimed that the potassium cyanide in the adulterated capsules was a corrosive that would quickly destroy the gelatin capsule-shells. Officials cited this alleged super-corrosive characteristic of cyanide as proof that the Tylenol capsules had been filled with cyanide and planted in the retail stores the day before the poisonings. But they really had no idea when or where the capsules had been tampered with.

The preliminary findings of a forensic analysis initiated by Cook County Medical Examiner Dr. Robert Stein indicated that the cyanide was not nearly as corrosive as officials suggested. Dr. Stein, when addressing the reporters at Mayor Byrne's Friday night news conference, described the early results of the test that was being conducted to detect approximately when the adulterated Tylenol capsules had been filled with cyanide. Stein said that he and his staff had emptied several Extra Strength Tylenol capsules on Thursday morning, and then refilled the capsules with cyanide from the cyanide-filled capsules in the Janus and Kellerman bottles. These test capsules showed no signs of corrosion 36 hours after they had been filled with cyanide.

The following day, Stein said that the cyanide could have remained in the adulterated capsules "for at least 48 hours" without revealing any "tell-tale" signs of their content. "We're at 48 hours now," said Stein. "[The test capsules] still look normal."

If these test capsules did not show signs of corrosion soon, the hypothesis that the cyanide would eat through the gelatin-based capsule-shells in just a couple days would be completely debunked. Also discredited, because of the timeframe involved, would be the theory that the tamperings had occurred at the retail stores. An analysis of the information known about the victim's bottles of cyanide-laced Tylenol further discredits the tampering-in-the-retail-stores hypothesis.

Of the seven poisoning victims, Mary McFarland was the outlier. She was the only one who did not die from her first dose taken from a bottle of cyanide-laced Tylenol capsules. McFarland had purchased her 50-count bottle of Extra Strength Tylenol probably on Tuesday, September 28th. The bottle contained seven cyanide-laced Tylenol capsules. None of the first five Tylenol capsules consumed by McFarland contained cyanide. When she took the sixth and seventh capsules in one dose on Wednesday evening, the odds caught up with her. One of those capsules did contain cyanide.

There must have been others like McFarland who also consumed Tylenol capsules from a bottle containing cyanide-laced capsules, but who took only the non-poisoned capsules and then heard the alerts and took no more. There also must have been people who bought bottles of poisoned Tylenol, but never even opened those bottles.

The first five Tylenol capsules that McFarland had taken from her new Tylenol bottle did not contain cyanide. That was a reasonable outcome, as the probability that one of those first five capsules would contain cyanide was about 54 percent (as calculated in the appendix). Conversely, it was extremely improbable that the first dose taken from each of the other victims' four bottles would all contain cyanide—but they all did. This was a nearly impossible outcome—unless there were many more bottles of cyanide-laced Tylenol in the Chicago area that the public never knew about.

Mary Kellerman and Paula Prince had each taken just one capsule from their bottles of Tylenol, whereas Lynn Reiner and Adam Janus had each taken two capsules from their bottles. The probability that the first dose consumed by these four victims would contain a cyanide-laced capsule can be determined from the available data, which includes the number of cyanide-laced capsules in each bottle, the total number of capsules in each bottle, and the number of capsules consumed by each victim.

The probability that the first dose taken from all four of the Kellerman, Janus, Reiner, and Prince Tylenol bottles would contain a cyanide-laced capsule was 0.0547 percent, or said another way: 1 in 1,828 (as calculated in the appendix). It is simply not plausible that the first dose taken from all four of those bottles would all contain cyanide, unless there were many other people who consumed Tylenol capsules from many other bottles of cyanide-laced Tylenol, but avoided the poisoned capsules.

There was about an 18 percent probability, on average, that the first dose taken from the Kellerman, Janus, Reiner, and Prince bottles would contain cyanide. If 20 Chicago-area residents each purchased one bottle containing cyanide-laced Tylenol capsules, then the probability that the first dose taken from four of those 20 bottles would contain cyanide is about 50 percent, calculated as follows:

> Binomial Distribution Calculation: Where the probability that the first dose taken will contain cyanide = 18%, the number of bottles opened and a dose consumed = 20, and the number of successes (i.e., the dose taken contains cyanide) = 4, then the probability that the first dose taken from 4 or more of those 20 bottles would contain cyanide equals 49.7 percent.

$$(x + a)^n = \sum_{k=0}^{n} \binom{n}{k} x^k a^{n-k} = 49.7\%$$

A reasonably conservative estimate is that about twenty Chicago-area residents each bought a bottle of cyanide-laced Tylenol and then took the first dose from those bottles during the 24-hour period when the victims' bottles of cyanide-laced Tylenol were purchased and the poisoned capsules consumed.

There were certainly other people who also bought bottles of cyanide-laced Tylenol capsules but did not consume any capsules from those bottles. If 50 percent of the Chicago area residents who bought bottles of Extra Strength Tylenol during the relevant 24-hour period did not consume any of their capsules, then Chicago area residents must have purchased approximately 40 bottles of cyanide-laced Tylenol, calculated as follows: 20 bottles / 50% = 40 bottles. This estimate of 40 poisoned bottles does not include the unsold bottles of poisoned Tylenol in Chicago area stores.

The Daily Herald reported that the first poisoned capsules to turn up during the inspection of Tylenol bottles in Chicago-area stores had been discovered on Friday, October 1st in at least two unsold bottles of Tylenol confiscated from the shelves of the Osco Drug store in Woodfield Mall in Schaumburg. *The New York Times* also reported that two unsold bottles of contaminated Tylenol had been recovered from the Schaumburg Osco Drug. Tyrone Fahner said that these bottles would be "particularly helpful, because they had not been sold and may provide some fingerprints."

Later that night, however, an FDA spokesperson said that seven cyanide-laced Tylenol capsules had been found in only one of the bottles removed from the Osco Drug store, and seven more capsules from that same bottle were suspect. Then, on Saturday, FDA spokesperson William Grigg said that investigators had found seven cyanide-filled Tylenol capsules in one of the bottles seized from the Osco Drug store, making no mention of the second bottle or the seven other suspect capsules. Officials had now inexplicably reduced the number of bottles of poisoned Tylenol recovered from Osco Drug to just one bottle.

Many years later, FDA Deputy Director Mark Novitch confirmed that two unsold bottles of cyanide-laced Tylenol had in fact been recovered from Osco Drug. Novitch said, "Two more poisoned containers were found on retail shelves during the sweep that followed [the Tylenol poisoning deaths]."

Two additional bottles of cyanide-laced Tylenol were discovered by Johnson & Johnson more than three weeks after the murders. Both of those bottles had been turned in by Chicago area residents.

Officially, there were eight bottles of cyanide-laced Tylenol recovered from the Chicago area. However, authorities intrinsically understood that there were other bottles of poisoned Tylenol that were never recovered.

FBI Special Agent Thomas Biebel, a member of the Tylenol task force, said, "We don't know how many other stores were involved. Probably a lot of people flushed [poisoned] Tylenol down the toilet."

NBC News later reported that authorities involved in the investigation felt that some contaminated capsules were lost due to the statement by Tyrone Fahner suggesting that people should destroy their Tylenol capsules. A survey conducted by Audits and Surveys, Inc. found that 60 percent of Chicago-area residents had in fact destroyed or discarded their Tylenol capsules during the first week after the poisonings.

A reasonable estimate of the number of bottles of cyanide-laced Tylenol in Chicago area stores can be deduced from information disclosed about the stores where bottles of poisoned Tylenol were purchased. Video clips taken by network news programs shortly after the murders showed various Jewel-Osco stores with about six to twelve bottles of Extra Strength Tylenol capsules in the front row of the stores' shelves. Some Jewel-Osco store managers told NBC News that they were selling one or two bottles of Extra Strength Tylenol capsules per day. Fahner said only one contaminated bottle had been found in each affected store, leading him to believe that the capsules had been planted at the front of the shelf.

Based on these assumptions, the probability of someone purchasing the one poisoned bottle from the front row of six to twelve bottles is around one in six, or 17 percent. In this scenario, an estimated 235 bottles of cyanide-laced Tylenol capsules were in Chicago-area stores on the day of the Tylenol murders, as calculated by dividing 40 (the estimated number of bottles of cyanide-laced Tylenol purchased) by 17 percent.

Could one man put hundreds of bottles of cyanide-laced Tylenol capsules on the shelves of dozens to a couple hundred Chicago area stores in one day without being caught? This hypothesis was not embraced by everyone.

In June 1983, Philip Corboy, the attorney who filed product liability lawsuits against J&J on behalf of Mary Kellerman and Mary McFarland, said, "The media did an excellent job of informing the public that a madman was out there, but I don't know of any evidence of that. Where along the line it happened is something a jury will decide." Unfortunately, a jury never got the opportunity to decide that issue.

As of October 8, 1982, Chicago Police Superintendent Richard Brzeczek had also not accepted the tampering in the retail stores theory as an established fact. "We're still in the process of trying to understand the scenario of events as to how the cyanide got into those bottles," he explained. "That's what you need to do to tie it in with a specific person."

Cook County Medical Examiner Dr. Robert Stein criticized officials for concentrating their efforts only on the tampering in the retail stores scenario. He said the Tylenol capsules could have been poisoned at their distribution point or at the plant where they were produced. Stein said the Tylenol killer struck him—not as a madman—but as more of a "rational evildoer."

10

A Cooperative Effort

For Johnson & Johnson, the theory that the tamperings had occurred during distribution was problematic, because in this scenario the company could have been held liable for the Tylenol murders. Under Title 21 of the U.S. Code of Federal Regulations, Johnson & Johnson was responsible for all aspects of manufacturing Tylenol, including all packaging and labeling operations, no matter where they were done.

Richard Epstein, a law professor at the University of Chicago and the author of several books on consumer law, explained the legal implications for J&J if the tamperings occurred in the retail stores, versus the distribution channel. "If the tampering is not linked to the manufacture or distribution of Tylenol," said Epstein, "McNeil could be free from any liability." If, however, it turned out that a disgruntled employee altered the capsules at the manufacturing plant or somewhere along the way before the bottles were shipped, Epstein said McNeil "would be in a lot more trouble."

Burke became so concerned about the Tylenol problem that he elevated the management of the crisis to the corporate level and took control of managing the company's response himself. "One of the things that was bothering me," said Burke, "is the extent to which Johnson & Johnson was becoming deeply involved in the affair. The public was learning that Tylenol was a Johnson & Johnson product, and the dilemma was how to protect the name and not incite whoever did this to attack other Johnson & Johnson products."

The FBI brought in John Douglas to develop a psychological profile of the Tylenol killer. Douglas, according to the biography on his web site, is the legendary head of the FBI Support Unit and a pioneer in developing profiles for some of the most notorious and sadistic criminals of our time, including the "Tylenol poisoner." At the time of the Tylenol murders, however, Douglas admittedly had no experience in this type of case.

In his book, *Mind Hunter*, Douglas says, "Despite the fact that this was early in my career and I'd never done a product tampering case before, nor had I ever interviewed a convicted tamperer in prison, it seemed to me that the killer would likely fit the development models we'd observed for other types of cowardly predators." Douglas said the Tylenol killer had not targeted a specific person or store, and there appeared to be no motive. "The country was witnessing a form of terrorism; someone, somewhere, could contaminate almost anything they bought and they would innocently consume it and die." Douglas said the Tylenol tampering was, therefore, a crime involving psychological distance.

Douglas said he believed that the killer was a man with a long history of failures in all areas of life who would probably have a record of complaints of injustices against him. He would have gravitated toward positions of authority, but would have had trouble keeping a job and likely had a psychiatric record. He would have had periods of depression and hopelessness, explained Douglas, and likely experienced some stressful event around the time when the deaths occurred late in September. Douglas said he would also be talkative about the news story to anyone who would listen.

Dawn Hobbs, a journalist who covered the criminal justice system in the 1980s, said the profile constructed of a Tylenol terrorist was criticized by some as being too general to be of any assistance in the investigation. In a criminal case that lacks evidence and involves a random selection of victims, like those in the Tylenol murders, the chances of constructing an accurate profile significantly diminish, said Hobbs. Nonetheless, she said a profile is often an essential tool that can assist investigators, at least to a certain degree, in their search for the perpetrator. On the other hand, said Hobbs, a criminal profile also has the ability to mislead an investigation.

Douglas's profile of the Tylenol killer, rooted in the notion that the tamperings occurred in the retail stores, may have misled the investigation by diverting the attention of police, consumers, and the press away from the distribution channel. This profile did not lead to the capture of the killer, and, in this regard, the Tylenol murders investigation failed completely. Yet James Burke gave a glowing assessment of the investigation.

Burke said, "The public was served well because of the extraordinary cooperation that occurred among all the responsible elements of society. The regulatory agencies, the wholesale and retail parts of the distribution system; the various medical professionals, the local federal and state law enforcement agencies...all worked together with the media to alert the public to the danger and to protect them in the process." The cooperation between J&J, the FBI, and the FDA was, according to Burke, "a demonstration without parallel of government and business working with the news media to help protect the public."

Johnson & Johnson established close relations with the Chicago police, the FBI, and the FDA. In this way, according to a public relations executive from Burson-Marsteller, the company could play a role in searching for the person who poisoned the Tylenol capsules and could help prevent further tamperings.

The rock-solid relationship that Johnson & Johnson had with the FBI began with its agents in Chicago and went all the way up to FBI Director William Webster. Larry Foster said J&J executives talked daily with officials at the crime scene and at both FBI and FDA headquarters. "Jim Burke spent much of the early days in Washington conferring with Arthur Hull Hayes, the FDA commissioner, and his staff, and with FBI Director William Webster and his staff."

Johnson & Johnson strengthened its ties with the FBI Office in Chicago by hiring Intertel Security Systems, a private detective agency in Norwood, Illinois, to investigate the Tylenol tamperings. Many of Intertel's private investigators were former FBI agents. J&J has routinely hired private investigators to remove certain Johnson & Johnson products from the marketplace. J&J hired private investigators and former FBI agents in the 1980s through the 2000s to track down and remove from the marketplace a variety of diverted J&J products, including diabetes test strips, toothbrushes, and Procrit (an anti-anemia drug). In the Tylenol murders case, J&J likely hired Intertel to track down all of the potentially poisoned Tylenol capsules so they could be destroyed.

Johnson & Johnson sent a contingent of security and public relations personnel to Chicago on the same morning the company's executives learned about the poisonings. "Bob Andrews [assistant director of public relations at J&J] spent maybe three to five weeks at the scene in Chicago, following the story day to day," said Larry Foster. "He knew the reporters that were covering [the story]. He knew the FBI and the other authorities who were working on the solution, and his information—the feedback—was invaluable."

The leaders of the Tylenol task force had reason to be sympathetic toward Johnson & Johnson, a corporation that operated more than a dozen plants in the Chicago area and brought thousands of jobs and hundreds-of-millions of dollars into the Illinois economy. The cooperation between Illinois officials and Johnson & Johnson was readily apparent on the second day of the investigation when, instead of inspecting the Tylenol capsules in the Chicago marketplace, authorities turned them over to Johnson & Johnson.

Fahner said that a J&J official had informed his office on Thursday, September 30th that Johnson & Johnson would pay all costs associated with collecting the Tylenol capsules from stores in Illinois and moving them to a temporary lab in Lemont, 26 miles southwest of Chicago. That lab, staffed with 30 J&J toxicologists, was set up by Johnson & Johnson in one of its own warehouses— the Johnson & Johnson Midwest Distribution Center.

On Friday, the second day of the investigation, IDLE Commander Edward Cisowski said the Lemont warehouse had already been cleared to store all of the Tylenol bottles turned over to police or confiscated from stores in the Chicago area. Johnson & Johnson had thus taken control of the physical evidence from the Tylenol murders crime scene and had also been given the responsibility of inspecting the Chicago-area Tylenol capsules.

11

Handling the Evidence

Chicago Mayor Jane Byrne held her second news conference about the Tylenol murders case on Saturday night, October 2nd. She ordered Chicago police and health officials to remove all Tylenol products from all 2,000 stores throughout the city by 6 p.m. the next day. That order did not sit well with the J&J executives who had already put a great deal of effort into assuring retailers, wholesalers, and consumers that the tamperings affected only Extra Strength Tylenol capsules.

Two days earlier, Johnson & Johnson had agreed to cover all costs associated with moving Tylenol capsules from the Chicago-area stores to the company's Lemont distribution center. However, when Mayor Byrne banned the sale of all Tylenol products—including Regular Strength Tylenol capsules—Johnson & Johnson reminded her that its offer to collect and inspect the Chicago-area Tylenol capsules applied only to Extra Strength Tylenol capsules.

In responding to Mayor Byrne's order to remove all Tylenol products from Chicago stores, J&J's local attorney, Paul Noland, said Johnson & Johnson would not pay to collect or inspect any Regular Strength Tylenol capsules. Noland further clarified that all Extra-Strength Tylenol capsules collected in the Chicago area were to be delivered only to Johnson & Johnson's distribution center in Lemont and inspected only by J&J employees. The FBI and Illinois officials agreed to these conditions.

To track down the facility where the tamperings actually occurred, authorities needed to collect the Tylenol capsules from all the Chicago-area outlets so they could be tested for cyanide. But authorities actually did the exact opposite of that. One of Johnson &

Johnson's own documents reveals that only an insignificant number of Tylenol capsules were actually inspected.

In a "Dear Doctor" letter, dated October 13, 1982, Dr. Thomas Gates, the medical director for McNeil Consumer Products, wrote:

> The Food and Drug Administration, the investigative authorities in the Chicago area, and McNeil Consumer Products Company scientists have collectively examined over 2 million individual capsules collected randomly throughout the country and have found no evidence of cyanide contamination.

The final number of inspected Tylenol capsules was two million, the same amount cited in J&J's October 13th Dear Doctor letter. FDA Deputy Commissioner Mark Novitch said the FDA had randomly tested 1.5 million Tylenol capsules, primarily from outside the Chicago area. Five-hundred thousand capsules were inspected from inside the Chicago area. Of those 500,000 Chicago-area capsules, the *New York Times* reported that more than 310,000 were tested by Chicago authorities, meaning J&J tested no more than 190,000 capsules. A United Press International story put the total number of capsules tested by J&J at 142,850. At 50 capsules per bottle, Johnson & Johnson tested between 2,857 and 3,800 bottles of Tylenol capsules out of just 10,000 bottles tested from the Chicago area and about 40,000 bottles tested nationwide.

There were about 165,000 retail outlets selling Tylenol products in the United States in 1982. About 11,000 were in the Chicago area. If each of the 11,000 Chicago-area stores had 20 bottles of Extra Strength Tylenol capsules on hand, then about 220,000 bottles were in Chicago area stores on the day of the murders. J&J toxicologists tested only 1.43 percent to 1.73 percent of those bottles and discovered two bottles that contained cyanide-laced capsules.

By late Saturday afternoon, October 2nd, Chicago-area residents had turned in more than 1,500 bottles of Tylenol to Chicago's northwest suburban police stations, and an unspecified number to authorities in Chicago. They continued to turn in Tylenol capsules for several more days. The few thousand bottles of Tylenol capsules inspected by J&J had evidently all been turned in by Chicago-area residents, meaning J&J did not inspect any of the Tylenol capsules from the Chicago-area stores, hospitals, repackaging facilities, or distribution centers.

Tyrone Fahner's first impulse was to get the Tylenol capsules off the shelves of Chicago-area stores and out of the homes of Chicago-area residents. Fahner's decision to turn over the Tylenol capsules to Johnson & Johnson on the first day of the investigation indicated that he had quickly dismissed the theory that the tamperings occurred at a repackaging facility or distribution center. Fahner simply assumed that the tamperings took place in the retail stores, so he allowed Johnson & Johnson to collect and destroy the capsules that could have been used by investigators to trace the poisoned capsules to a central point in the channel of distribution.

"We're trying to understand what kind of person could do these things," said Fahner. "It is an act of a random murderer who then placed [the cyanide-laced Tylenol capsules] in the stores."

Just two days into the investigation, the Tylenol task force had already developed a list of about two dozen suspects. "They range in age from a young hippie to an old man," said Fahner. The suspects at the top of Fahner's list were members of the victims' families. Statements by some of these relatives, and testimony given by local police officers during a coroner's inquest, reveal that the relatives who were considered suspects eventually took lie detector tests after being pressured to do so by authorities.

The Tylenol task force focused their investigative efforts on several notable occurances that they hoped would connect one of the victims' relatives to the murders. The Lynn Reiner case stood out because of the six red and white Extra Strength Tylenol capsules in her bottle of gray and white Regular Strength Tylenol capsules. Mary McFarland's cyanide-laced Extra Strength Tylenol capsules, because they were found in a Dristan bottle in her purse, also caught the attention of investigators. It was also odd that three members of the Janus family had all taken cyanide-laced Extra Strength Tylenol capsules from one 50-count bottle that had contained twelve poisoned capsules. These incidents, rather than the Tylenol capsules in the Chciago-area marketplace, were viewed by investigators as their best leads for solving the murders.

If government officials had wanted to inspect all of the Chicago-area Tylenol capsules, they could have easily done so. The capsule testing procedure consisted of dropping a cyanide-detecting strip of litmus paper into each Tylenol bottle tested and then checking the litmus paper a few minutes later to see if it had turned blue. If each of J&J's 30 toxicologists at the company's temporary lab in Lemont inspected two bottles per minute and worked twelve hours per day, then each could have tested 1,440 bottles per day. At this rate, they could have logically tested 43,220 bottles per day and 302,400 bottles per week. In the entire inspection period, however, J&J tested no more than 3,800 bottles of Extra Strength Tylenol capsules.

Authorities also could have used the imaging machine produced by Lixi Inc., of Downers Grove, Illinois to inspect the Tylenol capsules rapidly. The Lixi device, a low-intensity fluoroscope, could detect as little as 20 milligrams of "foreign matter" in a 500-milligram Tylenol capsule without removing the capsules from the bottles or boxes. Joseph E. Pascente, the president of Lixi, later said his fluoroscope was used by Bristol-Myers in October 1982 to screen for tainted Excedrin after a man in Denver swallowed an Excedrin capsule filled with mercuric chloride. Authorities in Seattle also used this device to inspect bottles of Excedrin and Anacin capsules after tampering incidents involving these products in June 1986. Pascente offered the Lixi device to Illinois authorities to search out the cyanide-laced Tylenol capsules, but he said "nobody listened."

The dubious nature of the Tylenol capsules inspection process was matched by what some low-level members of the Tylenol task force confidentially described as a farcical inspection of the McNeil plant in Fort Washington by Michael Schaffer, the Cook County chief toxicologist. Johnson & Johnson flew Schaffer in on Monday October 4th to conduct a half-day inspection of McNeil's 375,000 square-foot Tylenol manufacturing plant in Fort Washington. Schaffer spent a few hours at the sprawling plant before declaring, "No human hands touched the Tylenol or its ingredients in the automated mixing and packaging process."

"I don't think it's impossible," Schaffer added, "but it's a million to one [that the contamination occurred at the plant]."

Schaffer knew next to nothing about the manufacturing process for Tylenol, and he was unqualified to offer a relevant opinion about the location where the tamperings did or did not occur. He did not know how McNeil handled the raw materials used in making Tylenol, how the Tylenol was shipped, or how it was handled during distribution. Furthermore, no one ever explained where the Tylenol implicated in the poisonings had been stored from the time it was manufactured in the spring of 1982 until it was shipped to Illinois in late August 1982.

Officials were conspicuously silent about Johnson & Johnson's Tylenol distribution network. Spokespersons for J&J, the FDA, and the Tylenol task force never even mentioned the third party "rack jobbers" that delivered Tylenol to Chicago-area stores and pharmacies.

12

Rack Jobbers

The Daily News Record, in Harrisonburg, Virginia, reported on Saturday, October 2, 1982 that several bottles of Tylenol from a batch implicated in the Tylenol poisonings had been sold at an IGA supermarket in Bridgewater, Virginia. One of the store's customers said a bottle she purchased on Wednesday, September 29th bore the lot number MC2880, the same lot number that was on the Kellerman and Janus Tylenol bottles. Another woman had also returned a bottle with that same lot number to the Bridgewater IGA on Thursday night.

Jim Liptrap, the assistant manager of the Bridgewater IGA store, checked the store's shelves and discovered more bottles from Lot MC2880. He wasn't sure how many of the bottles from that lot had been on the shelf and had no way of knowing how many had been sold. He said that Sav-A-Stop, a nationally known rack jobber, "takes care of the ordering and stocking. We don't keep an inventory of that."

Rack jobbers are wholesale distribution companies that rent space in retail stores and supermarkets to display and sell products. The people who actually restock the display shelves are also called rack jobbers, or alternatively, merchandisers. Rack jobbers came into prominence in the grocery industry in the 1950s with the entry of supermarkets into non-food product-lines. They developed the "health and beauty care" category for a section of a supermarket or discount store that featured non-prescription drugs and a variety of other products, previously sold primarily in pharmacies. Rack jobbers provide retailers the opportunity to earn additional revenue while relieving them of all responsibility for warehousing, reordering, and re-stocking the products. The rack jobbers create the displays, guarantee the sale of all merchandise, and re-stock the displays. In return, the supermarket supplies the space and collects a percentage of the gross sales.

Ann Saylor, the manager of the IGA store in Grottoes, Virginia, said representatives from Sav-A-Stop had told her that none of the Tylenol delivered to Grottoes was from the suspect batches. But when IGA employees checked their inventory, she said they found ten bottles with the MC2880 lot number. These suspect Tylenol bottles came from Sav-A-Stop's warehouse in Salem, Virginia.

The general manager of Sav-A-Stop's Salem warehouse, Howard Quoss, said that he had no idea how many bottles from the lots implicated in the Tylenol poisonings had been supplied to area stores. "Lot numbers are not listed on supply invoices that Sav-A-Stop receives from McNeil," he said.

Spokespersons for Kroger and Safeway said their stores in Virginia and elsewhere also received Tylenol from Sav-A-Stop. A Kroger official said 14 Tylenol bottles from lot number MC2880 were found in the chain's Roanoke, Virginia stores. A Safeway spokesperson said the company's stores in North Carolina and central Virginia had sold an unknown number of bottles from Lot MC2880.

Safeway and Kroger, the two largest supermarket chains in the nation in 1982, and IGA, the largest group of independent supermarkets, relied on rack jobbers to order and restock their stores with Tylenol and other health and beauty care products. The industry-wide use of rack jobbers to restock stores with OTC drugs like Tylenol did not align with the distribution process espoused by spokespersons from J&J and the FDA who said full cases of 72 bottles of Tylenol capsules were shipped unopened, directly from the McNeil manufacturing plants to the retailers' warehouses.

According to *Newsweek*, many experts thought it was unlikely that any tampering occurred along the distribution chain, as the packages of Tylenol were shrink-wrapped in plastic in groups of six at the factory, and adulterating individual bottles before they reached retail stores would be readily apparent from the broken wrapping. FDA Deputy Commissioner Mark Novitch said the Tylenol bottles were wrapped in plastic and put in cartons as they left the factory and remained that way until the retailers received them. "If a retailer had received an open package in which a bottle had been removed and tampered with, it would become immediately obvious," said Novitch.

But that wasn't really true. The cases of 72 Tylenol bottles were typically opened, and the plastic-wrap torn off the 12 six-packs of Tylenol bottles before rack jobbers such as Sav-A-Stop delivered the Tylenol bottles to retail stores.

Sav-A-Stop, a privately held company headquartered in Jacksonville, Florida, had annual sales of $250 million and was one of the nation's largest rack jobbers, supplying some 18,000 health and beauty care products to 9,500 supermarkets and convenience stores nationwide. Sav-A-Stop described itself in a 1966 trademark registration with the U.S. Patent Office as follows:

> For: Rack jobbing services – Namely filling and stocking shelves of various retail stores with sundry and drug merchandise manufactured by others, maintaining inventory, accounting and tax records for such stores, and advertising such merchandise displayed and sold from such stocked shelves.

Sav-A-Stop supplied Tylenol to supermarkets, drugstores, and mass merchandisers throughout the country, including the Chicago area. On July 30, 1982, two months before the Tylenol murders, Sav-A-Stop had run a help-wanted ad in the *Daily Herald*, seeking a non-food merchandiser for a number of stores in Chicago's northwest suburban area. The ad read:

> The nation's leading non-food merchandiser, Sav-A-Stop, Inc., is in need of permanent part-time help in Woodfield [Mall], Spring Hill Mall, Stratford Square, Hawthorne Center, Northbrook Court, Deerbrook Mall - to merchandise health and beauty aids in major Department Stores. Duties include writing orders, merchandising and maintaining shelves.

The distribution of Tylenol by rack jobbers provides an explanation of how so many bottles of cyanide-laced Tylenol capsules could have turned up in Chicago-area stores all at the same time. Sometime before the murders, one or more rack jobbers, working their normal sales routes, likely restocked the display shelves of dozens or hundreds of Chicago-area stores with bottles of Extra Strength Tylenol capsules.

Officials surmised that the Tylenol killer had driven Highways 90/94, 290, and 294, following a near circular route. They further concluded that the killer had probably placed the tampered products on store shelves on Tuesday afternoon, September 28th, suggesting that he had no daytime employment or at least no full-time employment. However, this daytime delivery actually suggested that the bottles containing cyanide-laced Tylenol capsules had been delivered to the stores by gainfully employed rack jobbers.

Government officials and J&J executives never talked publicly about the distributors that received, stored, and delivered Tylenol to retailers, institutional pharmacies, and secondary distributors. They also never mentioned the third party repackagers that bottled and packaged Tylenol. Nevertheless, the large amount of Tylenol in the distribution system at the time of the murders indicated that most of that Tylenol had been shipped from the McNeil plants in bulk containers of Tylenol capsules or powder and then bottled and packaged later by repackagers.

J&J spokesperson Robert Kniffin said there were 11 million bottles of Tylenol capsules (Regular Strength and Extra Strength) in the U.S. distribution system at the time of the Tylenol murders. However, after a second Tylenol tampering incident 40 months later, in 1986, Joseph Chiesa, the president of McNeil Consumer Products, said there were then only about one million bottles of Tylenol capsules (Regular Strength and Extra Strength) in the distribution system. The amount of Tylenol capsules sold in 1982 and 1986 was similar, so it made no sense that there were eleven times as many Tylenol capsules in the distribution channel in October of 1982 as there were in February of 1986.

Annual Tylenol sales were $450 million in 1982 and $525 million in 1986, of which about 30 percent came from capsules. At $3.60 per bottle in 1982 and $3.70 per bottle in 1986, J&J was selling about 772,000 bottles of Tylenol capsules per week in 1982 and about 811,000 bottles per week in 1986.

The one million bottles of Tylenol capsules that J&J said were in the distribution channel in February of 1986 represented nine days, or about 1.23 weeks of supply. Whereas the 11 million bottles of Tylenol capsules J&J said were in the distribution channel in October of 1982 represented a whopping 107 days, or about 15.23 weeks of supply. Wholesalers would not have stored anywhere near 15 weeks of supply of bottled Tylenol capsules.

Pharmaceutical wholesalers typically carry enough of a given product to cover less than one month's worth of sales. Food and drug stores also keep low inventory levels of non-food products on hand, enough to cover less than two weeks of sales. There should have been no more than about four to six weeks of supply of Tylenol capsules in the distribution channel in September 1982. There were certainly not 11 million bottles of Tylenol capsules (constituting more than 15 weeks of sales) in the distribution channel. Rather, there was enough Tylenol powder or capsules in the distribution channel to *fill* 11 million bottles with Tylenol capsules. Some of that Tylenol had already been bottled, but much of it was in bulk containers sitting in repackaging facilities waiting to be bottled and packaged.

An "FDA Alert" regarding a shipment of bulk Tylenol in 2001 provides a glimpse of what was also going on with the packaging of Tylenol in 1982. This alert said that on June 28, 2001, the FDA's district office in San Juan, Puerto Rico monitored the destruction of 16 drums of Tylenol 80mg Fruit Chewable Tablets that had been manufactured at McNeil's plant in Las Piedras, Puerto Rico. The bulk containers of Tylenol had arrived at the San Juan port on April 22, 2000 and stood unclaimed by McNeil for over a year. The U.S. Customs Service, interested in auctioning off the Tylenol, contacted the FDA. A subsequent investigation found that the Tylenol tablets had been shipped to Canada to undergo the packaging process, but were returned intact because the repackager was unable to complete the process before the product expiration date.

In 1982, just as in 2001, not all Tylenol was bottled at McNeil's manufacturing plants. Some was shipped to third-party repackagers that bottled the Tylenol. FDA officials said the tamperings did not occur at the McNeil manufacturing plants, but they never said the tamperings did not occur at a repackaging facility or at a distribution center.

13

A Reluctant Recall

On Monday, October 4th, reporters got a chance to question Al Swanson and Joseph Chavez, the Kane County deputies who had found the boxes of Extra Strength Tylenol capsules in the Elgin Howard Johnson's parking lot 28 1/2 hours before the poisonings began. The deputies had learned about the Tylenol murders one day after they occurred, and officials from the Tylenol task force and the Kane County Sheriff's Office had gone out to the Howard Johnson's on Friday, October 1st, but the cartons of Tylenol capsules were gone.

Sergeant David Burrows, of the Kane County Sheriff's Office, said most of the capsule-parts still in the parking lot had been run over and crushed in the ensuing two days. He said they did however send 31 capsules Friday morning by registered mail to the State Department of Public Health's toxicology lab in Chicago. The result from the analysis of those capsules was never disclosed.

On Monday, Deputy Sheriff Cole answered reporters' questions about the boxes that Chavez and Swanson had found in the Howard Johnson's parking lot. The interview was conducted over the phone, with Cole relaying the reporters' questions to Chavez and Swanson, who were on separate telephone lines.

The boxes "said Tylenol on them and one of them was open," recalled Deputy Chavez. "I picked up the powder," he said. "It looked like hundreds of capsules had been emptied. We looked at them and found a couple of capsules had been put [back] together."

Because Tylenol was not a controlled substance, the officers did not report the incident. "We just blew it off," said Chavez. "We just didn't think anything about it."

"It was evident [that the capsules] were tampered with," added Cole. "Some of the capsules were empty. They had no powder in them. The officers assumed there evidently was something going on with drugs," Cole explained.

Cole said the officers experienced dizziness, nausea, and vomiting minutes after handling the capsules. Swanson became so violently ill that he was relieved from his shift. Chavez had also become sick, but stayed on the clock until the end of the shift. He did not return to work until several days later. Dr. Barry Rumack, of the Rocky Mountain Poison Control Center in Denver, said, "The symptoms reported by the officers are consistent with cyanide poisoning."

"I was stupid," said Chavez. "I should have picked [the boxes of Tylenol] up and brought [them] in. I kick myself in the head every time I think of it. Maybe we could have saved these people's lives, or at least got an investigation started."

FBI agents questioned employees at the Howard Johnson's restaurant again on Monday morning, October 4th. The motel bookkeeper said people working on the case had asked for and received a list of guests, but she declined to say what time period the list covered. The media attention was wearing thin on at least one Howard Johnson's employee. "I wish you guys would stop bugging me," a manager at the restaurant told an Associated Press reporter. "I didn't see nothing."

The Tylenol cases that had been in the Howard Johnson's parking lot were the kind found at repackaging facilities and distribution centers. Whoever left those cases in the parking lot had access to Tylenol in the distribution channel. The best way to get the cyanide-laced Tylenol capsules into the retail stores was for the killer to simply plant them in a repackaging facility or distribution center so that a truck driver or rack jobber would unknowingly deliver them to retail stores and hospitals.

While FBI agents were questioning employees at the Howard Johnson restaurant on Monday morning, the members of J&J's Emergency Strategy Group were meeting in the company's corporate boardroom, reportedly to discuss the merits of a nationwide recall of all Tylenol capsules. J&J President David Clare said the climate within Johnson & Johnson at that time was one of sheer disbelief and incredulity that this had happened. There was "absolute unhappiness associated with the obvious fact that people were dying, potentially through the use of one of our products, and we just didn't know what had happened," explained Clare. "We did not know how extensive it was, what the cause was, what the problem was in any dimension. It appeared to be localized, but we weren't sure."

For a period of about 48 to 72 hours, said Clare, there was a debate within Johnson & Johnson as to whether or not the Tylenol capsules should be withdrawn from the market. "So there was the argument," recalled Clare, "We should not withdraw [Tylenol capsules from the market]—'You're going to enhance the copycats. You're going to enhance the process of adulterating a product for copycats.' And [we] finally came down on the side [that] there was no choice from our standpoint. We had to act to protect the public, whether it was more widespread than it appeared to be, whether it was a condition that could be repeated by other copycats using our product. So the first and foremost, we had to protect the public."

Clare's suggestion that he and his fellow executives had agreed to recall Tylenol capsules within 72 hours of learning about the poisonings was inaccurate. When the debate among the Emergency Strategy Group members ended on Monday morning, five days after the Tylenol murders, they had decided *not* to withdraw Tylenol capsules from the market. With this decision made, James Burke and Wayne Nelson hopped on the company helicopter and flew to Washington D.C. on Monday afternoon to meet with FBI and FDA officials there.

Burke and Nelson were in their second day of meetings in Washington D.C. when reports hit the newswire of another Tylenol poisoning—this time in California. Greg Blagg, a 27-year-old butcher from Oroville, California, told reporters on Tuesday afternoon that he had taken three Extra Strength Tylenol capsules on Thursday, September 30th and then passed out. Blagg said his wife had purchased the Tylenol two weeks earlier at Longs drugstore in Oroville.

His wife, Terry, drove him to the hospital where he was treated and released at his own request four hours later. Blagg said he heard on the news that night about the deaths in Chicago, and the next day he took apart some of the capsules from his own Tylenol bottle and saw pink flecks in the powder. He then turned the bottle over to his physician, Dr. John Clay. That evening, at Dr. Clay's suggestion, the Blaggs returned to the Longs drugstore in Oroville where they had purchased the original bottle, and bought two more bottles of Extra Strength Tylenol capsules.

Dr. Clay called Johnson & Johnson on Friday, October 1st, and alerted them to Blagg's contaminated Tylenol capsules. A J&J official told Dr. Clay to send the Tylenol capsules to McNeil's lab in Fort Washington. Late Monday night McNeil toxicologists completed the analysis of the Oroville Tylenol capsules and identified strychnine in two of the Blaggs' three bottles. At that point, said Larry Foster, the FDA was immediately notified.

As it turned out, Blagg's strychnine-laced Tylenol capsules were not planted by a would-be-killer. The press conference in Chicago to announce the deaths of three Tylenol poisoning victims was held at 8 a.m. (6 a.m. California time) on Thursday, September 30th. Blagg didn't go to the hospital until Thursday afternoon. Officials in California were suspicious of Blagg's story from the start. Blagg and his wife, Terry, agreed to take lie detector tests when police suggested that there were "discrepancies" in their story. The FBI officially closed the Oroville tampering case about two months later without prosecution.

*****

When the Oroville tampering incident made headline news, Burke recognized that his only viable option for curtailing the growing damage to the Tylenol brand was to recall all Tylenol capsules nationwide. Burke said that when he met with FDA and FBI officials in Washington D.C. on October 4th and 5th, he advocated for a recall of all Extra Strength Tylenol capsules. Burke said that the federal officials then counseled him against recalling the drug precipitously. "The FBI didn't want us to do it," explained Burke, "because it would say to whoever did this: 'Hey, I'm winning.

I can bring a major corporation to its knees.' And the FDA argued that a recall might cause more public anxiety than it would relieve."

Burke's suggestion that he was the lone voice fighting on behalf of American consumers to remove all Tylenol capsules from the marketplace is refuted by the facts. Prior to Burke's meeting with federal officials in Washington, J&J executives had already decided not to initiate a national recall of all Tylenol capsules.

The story about the strychnine-laced Tylenol poisoning in Oroville was made public on Tuesday, October 5th. But Burke had known about this incident since Friday, October 1st. He ordered the nationwide recall of all Tylenol capsules on Tuesday, not because he had just learned about the Tylenol tampering in Oroville, but because the public had just learned about the Tylenol tampering in Oroville.

The recall of two Tylenol lots on September 30th and October 1st were well publicized. Not publicized, however, were the other five lots linked to poisoned Tylenol capsules that Burke had not recalled.

Police had said Lynn Reiner's Tylenol capsules were in a bottle bearing the lot number 1833MB, but Tylenol from that lot was not recalled. The cyanide-laced Tylenol that killed Paula Prince was from Lot 1801MA, but Tylenol from that lot was not recalled. Authorities had also found cyanide in Extra Strength Tylenol capsules from Lots 1665LM and MC2884, but Burke refused to recall Tylenol from either of those lots. Strychnine-laced Tylenol capsules from yet another lot had been found in two bottles in California, but Burke did not recall Tylenol from that lot. By the end of the second day of the investigation, authorities had linked poisoned Extra Strength Tylenol capsules to seven different lot numbers, but Burke recalled Tylenol capsules from only two of those lots.

The nationwide recall of all Tylenol capsules was announced Tuesday afternoon, October 5th by a McNeil spokesperson who stated, "In conjunction with the FDA, we are notifying retailers to discontinue the sale of Tylenol extra strength capsules and regular strength capsules throughout the country until further notice."

The next morning, David Collins appeared on NBC's *Today* show, partly to mention the Tylenol recall, but mostly to tell the public that the poisonings were the work of a madman. "The confidence of the American consumer built this product. Nothing has changed," proclaimed Collins. "What has changed," he said, "is that we have an insane individual or individuals out there who have elected to contaminate this product...and we hope to reemphasize and reestablish consumers' confidence in this product."

In a lawsuit filed against its insurers to recover the costs of the recall, J&J suggested that the company's executives had treated the recall with far greater urgency than they actually had. Judge Maryanne Trump Barry, the older sister of real estate magnate Donald Trump, presided over this lawsuit. She said the "Plaintiff [J&J] itself admits, both in its complaint and in its briefs, that it would have been negligent or grossly negligent were any subsequent deaths caused by its retention of Tylenol on the market. It is a well settled proposition of law that an actor who has negligently imperiled the life of another has a duty to aid that person and save him or her if at all possible."

J&J argued that company executives, to avoid an even greater catastrophe, acted immediately to recall all of the Tylenol capsules. The transcript in McNeilab Inc. v. North River Insurance Co., et al. includes an interesting exchange regarding Johnson & Johnson's after-the-fact reason for recalling all Tylenol capsules nationwide:

> THE COURT: Well, what catastrophe were you stopping here?
>
> COUNSEL FOR J&J: Stopping the death of the additional unknown numbers of people.
>
> THE COURT: And that's why you did it?
>
> COUNSEL FOR J&J: That is a principal motivating factor for why we did it.

Judge Barry said, "[McNeil] and its parent [J&J] admit that they foresaw further poisoning incidents if they failed to act."

Yet, for six days, J&J executives had resisted the nationwide recall of all Tylenol capsules, hoping to get away with a piecemeal recall of Tylenol from just two lots. J&J did not recall all Tylenol capsules nationwide until five days after they had learned about the poisonings.

Even so, James Burke was not so careless that he would risk leaving cyanide-laced Tylenol capsules in stores and warehouses where they could get into the hands of consumers and cause even more deaths. By the time J&J executives initiated the national recall, they apparently had already tracked down the facility where the tamperings occurred and confiscated the Extra Strength Tylenol capsules that had been shipped from that warehouse.

J&J executives seemed to understand all along that only Extra Strength Tylenol capsules had been poisoned. Instead of warning consumers to avoid both Extra Strength and Regular Strength Tylenol capsules, J&J assured the public that *only* Extra Strength Tylenol capsules had been poisoned. The mailgrams that J&J had initially faxed to retailers, wholesalers, and doctors alerted them to the possible tampering of only Extra Strength Tylenol capsules.

When Chicago Mayor Jane Byrne announced that all Tylenol products were being removed from the city's 2,000 stores, Johnson & Johnson responded by refusing to collect or inspect any Regular Strength Tylenol capsules.

Larry Foster told reporters on October 4th that Johnson & Johnson had "temporarily suspended production of only Extra-Strength Tylenol [capsules], but all other Tylenol products are unaffected." If J&J executives truly believed that the tamperings occurred in the retail stores—they should have had no reason to believe that the Tylenol killer had not also planted cyanide-laced *Regular Strength* Tylenol capsules in Chicago area stores.

In a "Dear Doctor" letter to doctors, hospitals, and drug distributors, McNeil Medical Director Dr. Thomas Gates wrote: "There is widespread public confusion about which Tylenol products are involved. Many people do not understand that only Extra-Strength Tylenol Capsules have been implicated." This contention, however, was not entirely true.

J&J executives had learned on the day after the murders that a bottle of Regular Strength Tylenol—Lynn Reiner's bottle—did contain cyanide-laced Tylenol capsules. Inside Reiner's bottle of Regular Strength Tylenol capsules were six Extra Strength Tylenol capsules, four filled with cyanide. J&J executives could not have known that other bottles of Regular Strength Tylenol did not also contain cyanide-laced capsules—unless they knew that the Tylenol killer had not actually gone store to store to put the cyanide-laced Tylenol capsules into bottles sitting on the stores' shelves.

14

Vanishing Lot Numbers

Officials never disclosed the lot number for Lynn Reiner's cyanide-laced Extra Strength Tylenol capsules. Nor did they disclose the lot number for the second unsold bottle of cyanide-laced Tylenol recovered from the Osco Drug store. However, officials did identify two lot numbers—1665LM and MC2884—that were never publicly linked to a store or a victim. These two lot numbers were evidently from Lynn Reiner's package of cyanide-laced Extra Strength Tylenol capsules and the second bottle of cyanide-laced Tylenol from the Osco Drug store in Woodfield Mall.

As of Friday evening, October 1st, authorities had publicized the lot numbers for cyanide-laced Tylenol capsules from lots MC2880 and 1910MD only. That changed Friday night when, at the request of officials from the Tylenol task force, NBC's Chicago affiliate, WMAQ-TV, warned Chicago area residents that cyanide had been found in Extra Strength Tylenol from four different lots. In its 10 p.m. news broadcast on Friday, October 1st, WMAQ-TV announced:

> The task force is asking for help in solving the bizarre crime. They want those who still have Tylenol capsules from any of four lots to turn them over to their local police departments, or at least to the stores from which they were purchased. Those lots are labeled MC2880, MC2884, 1910MD, and 1665LM. Capsules are being tested around the clock for contamination and could provide valuable new leads in the case.

The local Arlington Heights newspaper, *The Daily Herald*, reported that the potential contamination had broadened Friday, as the poison had been found in three new batches of pills. These batches, 1910MD, 1665LM and MC2884, were added to the danger list on Friday, reported *The Daily Herald*. No national news outlet ever reported on the cyanide-laced Tylenol from lots MC2884 and 1665LM.

Late Friday night, officials said the cyanide-laced Tylenol that killed Paula Prince was from lot 1801MA. Authorities had now publicly linked the cyanide-laced Extra Strength Tylenol capsules from their specific lot numbers to each of the poisoning victims, with the exception of Lynn Reiner. The cyanide-laced Tylenol that killed Mary Kellerman and the Januses was from lot MC2880. The poisoned Tylenol that killed Mary McFarland was from lot 1910MD. And the cyanide-laced Tylenol that killed Paula Prince was from lot 1801MA.

For a number of reasons, Lynn Reiner's cyanide-laced Extra Strength Tylenol capsules probably came from lot 1665LM, rather than lot MC2884. Tylenol from lot MC2884 had been manufactured at McNeil's Fort Washington plant in the spring of 1982. The Tylenol from lot 1665LM had been manufactured at McNeil's Round Rock plant in 1981. McNeil sold the Tylenol from lot 1665LM under an NDC (National Drug Code) for unit-dose Extra Strength Tylenol capsules, which wholesalers distributed in containers of 100 to 1,000 capsules only to hospitals and other institutional pharmacies. The Tylenol from lot MC2884, since it was sold under the NDC for 50-count bottles of Extra Strength Tylenol capsules, was distributed to retailers.

Tylenol from lot MC2884 must have been in the second contaminated bottle found at the Osco Drug store, whereas Lynn Reiner's cyanide-laced Extra Strength Tylenol capsules must have been from lot 1665LM. The Tylenol from both these lots was shipped to an Illinois warehouse through J&J's regional distribution center in Montgomeryville, Pennsylvania.

On Saturday, October 2nd, lot numbers 1665LM and MC2884 were inexplicably removed from the danger list of cyanide-laced Tylenol lot numbers. The danger list now included only three lot numbers: MC2880, 1910MD, and 1801MA.

On Sunday, October 3rd, police—probably the Winfield police—told reporters for *The Daily Herald* and the Associated Press that they had identified a fourth lot number involved in the deaths. Police said Lynn Reiner had capsules from Lot 1833MB. This lot number, however, was from Lynn's bottle of *Regular Strength* Tylenol capsules. Lynn's coroner's report confirms that "one bottle labeled Regular Strength Tylenol, lot 1833MB," was submitted to the lab by DuPage County Chief Deputy Coroner Peter Siekmann on Thursday, September 30th.

Interestingly, police did not say that Lynn had *taken* Tylenol capsules from lot 1833MB, only that she *had* capsules from lot 1833MB. Police explained that there had been "initial confusion over the lot number" in the Lynn Reiner case because "she apparently had mixed Extra-Strength Tylenol capsules with her Regular Strength Tylenol capsules." Obviously, there could only have been confusion if there were two lot numbers to confuse. Yet with one brief news release, authorities had effectively replaced lot number 1665LM with lot number 1833MB, thus covering up the lot number of the poisoned Extra Strength Tylenol capsule that had caused the death of Lynn Reiner.

The official story of a madman who had planted the cyanide-laced Tylenol capsules in random Chicago area retail stores was not applicable to the Lynn Reiner case. Lynn's cyanide-laced Tylenol capsules had come from the closed-door pharmacy at Central DuPage Hospital. If authorities had admitted that Lynn's Extra Strength Tylenol had come from Central DuPage Hospital, then they also would have had to admit that the madman-in-the-retail-stores hypothesis had been debunked. Instead, the authorities removed the lot number for Lynn's Extra Strength Tylenol from the danger list and then proceeded with the investigation as though that lot number had never existed.

Winfield Police Officer Scott Watkins was the officer principally responsible for investigating the murder of Lynn Reiner. Watkins, now a lieutenant in the Lombard Police Department, was asked on August 19, 2010 what he knew about the investigation of Central DuPage Hospital as the probable source of Lynn Reiner's cyanide-laced Extra Strength Tylenol capsules.

Watkins said he was unaware of any such investigation.

When pressed further to offer some insight about the investigation that certainly must have included Central DuPage Hospital, Watkins shrugged his shoulders. It was the view of officials at that time, he said, that the tamperings were done at the retail stores.

When asked how authorities were able to determine that Lynn's Extra Strength Tylenol capsules were from lot LM1665, Watkins replied, "I don't know."

Watkins also said that on Thursday morning, September 30, 1982 he and other investigators had searched through Reiner's trash can and recovered the box for Lynn's bottle of Regular Strength Tylenol. That trash can is probably also where they found the unit-dose package for Lynn's Extra Strength Tylenol capsules. Printed on Lynn's unit dose package were the lot number of her Extra Strength Tylenol capsules and the name of the Central DuPage Hospital pharmacy where they had been dispensed. Officials never disclosed the name of the distributor that delivered the poisoned Tylenol capsules to Central DuPage Hospital, but they did spend a great deal of time questioning employees at the largest distributor of Tylenol to hospitals in the Chicago area—the Louis Zahn Drug Company.

15

Zahn Drug

When Central DuPage Hospital converted its pharmacy to a unit-dose system in 1974, it also contracted with a local distributor to manage its inventory and provide frequent deliveries of drugs and other products to its pharmacy. Distributors make "just in time" shipments to hospital pharmacies, usually several times per week. This system allows pharmacies to keep very low inventory levels and thus reduce costs. The distribution company that had the pharmacy-service-provider contract for Central DuPage Hospital delivered the cyanide-laced Extra Strength Tylenol capsules to the hospital's pharmacy.

On October 1st, and again on October 6th, 1982, ABC News showed video footage of cases containing seventy-two 50-count bottles of Extra Strength Tylenol capsules inside the Louis Zahn Drug Company's Melrose Park warehouse. Those Tylenol cases were just like the ones Al Swanson and Joseph Chavez had found in the parking lot at the Howard Johnson's Motor Lodge and Restaurant in Elgin 28 hours before the murders began. Cartons of Extra Strength Tylenol capsules were also in many other warehouses in Illinois at that time, but the Louis Zahn Drug Company was the pharmacy service provider that likely delivered the cyanide-laced Extra Strength Tylenol capsules to Central DuPage Hospital.

Louis Zahn founded the Louis Zahn Drug Company (Zahn Drug) in Melrose Park, Illinois in 1931. Zahn was a well-known business leader in Chicago and a long-time resident of Oak Park when he died in 1976, leaving the majority ownership of Zahn Drug to his son, Melvyn Zahn, who ran the company until 1989.

Zahn Drug, with $200 million in annual sales, was the largest independent drug wholesaler in the Midwest. It provided warehousing, merchandising, and purchasing management services to retail and institutional pharmacies, and carried prescription and OTC drugs, healthcare products, and a variety of other items normally stocked in drugstores. The company maintained its own delivery operation; leasing trucks and hiring union drivers to deliver drugs and healthcare products to pharmacies, retail stores, nursing homes, and hospitals. The company's headquarters and primary distribution center were located at 1930 George Street, five blocks east of Jewel's Melrose Park distribution center and about five blocks southeast of Jewel's repackaging and distribution warehouse in Franklin Park.

In 1982, Zahn Drug operated a state-of-the-art automated order picking system at its Melrose Park headquarters. The company's "Itematic" order fulfillment system was designed for extremely high throughput of a relatively small number of Stock Keeping Units. The Itematic was one of the most advanced systems of the time, with the capacity to select and deliver a variety of products in less than full-case quantities. Each customer's order was entered into the system's computer, and the system then automatically delivered the items to a workstation where they were manually picked (taken out of the bin) by a warehouse employee. The system used a number of rotating carousels, each having four columns of ten bins. The carousels moved along an oval track to the picking station and then rotated so the bin holding the appropriate item faced the human operator. A light on the bin containing the ordered item lit up, and the warehouse employee picked the item from the lit bin and placed it into a tote (a plastic container). This process was repeated until all items from the order were picked and placed into the tote. The tote, containing the products and a shipping document, was then sent down a conveyor belt to a packing station. A warehouse employee packaged the items in a carton that was then loaded onto a delivery truck.

The capacity of the system at Zahn Drug was approximately 1,600 orders per day with 53 pieces per order; a rate of 850 items per hour for each of the 12 Itematic picking machines in the system. The 12 machines each contained about 8,000 items typical of those found at the corner drugstore. The system selected or "picked" items, such as bottles, cassettes, vials, and other individually packaged items. The system's carousel-bins had to be manually replenished.

The video footage shown on ABC-News of the Zahn Drug warehouse showed only the area where the cases of Tylenol bottles were stored. It did not show the company's 12 automated picking machines or the company's employees manually loading the picking machines and filling individual stores' orders. Based on the video footage shown on ABC, it appeared that everything was just as J&J and the FDA had claimed. It looked like Zahn Drug received cases of 72 bottles of Extra Strength Tylenol capsules from McNeil, and then shipped those cases, unopened, to retail stores and hospitals. But that's not how the process actually worked.

In reality, warehouse employees opened the Tylenol cases and put the individual Tylenol bottles into the appropriate bins in the picking machines' carousels. A second employee, a "picker," placed the Tylenol bottles from each order into a tote. Then, a third employee, working at the packing station, manually handled the Tylenol bottles again as he placed the ordered items into boxes to be delivered to local retail stores and hospitals. Zahn Drug filled orders for Tylenol in multiples of one bottle—not in full cases of 72 bottles as Johnson & Johnson and the FDA led the public to believe.

Bottles of Extra Strength Tylenol capsules were rarely delivered to retail customers by the full case of 72 bottles. Rather, they were delivered in multiples of one Tylenol bottle. Most retail stores and hospital pharmacies received just-in-time deliveries of just enough Tylenol bottles to cover sales until the next shipment arrived, typically, no more than a week later.

The 165,000 stores nationwide that stocked Tylenol products sold an average of one or two bottles of Extra Strength Tylenol capsules per week. They did not order full cases of 72 Tylenol bottles. Most stores left the ordering of Tylenol and other health and beauty care products to rack jobbers and merchandisers who manually restocked the stores' shelves about once per week with just enough Tylenol bottles to fill the displays.

Zahn Drug served 1,400 drugstores in Illinois, Wisconsin, and Indiana. The company had formed a network of 50 independent charter pharmacies in 1974 called Family Drug Centers. The Family Drug Center (FDC) stores, located throughout the Greater Chicago area from the Illinois-Wisconsin border to Logansport, Indiana, had grown to 75 members in 1982; ten were in the Northwest suburbs of Chicago.

The communications between McNeil officials and the owner of Kesling Drug, Zahn Drug's FDC affiliate in Logansport, Indiana, indicated that McNeil executives believed Zahn Drug had handled some or all of the cyanide-laced Tylenol capsules. Most pharmacies never received a single call from J&J or McNeil officials regarding the Tylenol tamperings. Kesling Drug, however, received a great deal of attention from McNeil—an inordinate amount of attention in fact.

On the morning Johnson & Johnson learned about the Tylenol poisonings, a McNeil official called the owner of Kesling Drug and told her to remove all the bottles of Extra Strength Tylenol capsules from the store's shelves. Yet, on that same day, J&J executives told the general public that the tampering problem affected only a few stores in the Chicago area. Kesling Drug, located 133 miles southeast of Chicago was by no means in the Chicago area. So it was odd, even suspicious, that J&J was so concerned about getting the Tylenol capsules out of the Kesling Drug store.

On Friday, October 1st, David Maroney, of the Logansport *Pharos-Tribune*, interviewed Estel Kesling, the owner of Kesling Drug. Estel described the urgent calls she had received from McNeil executives the previous morning. "People started calling yesterday (Thursday), and we took [the Tylenol capsules] all off the shelf," Estel remarked. "McNeil already has called us twice on this. They made us go out and personally check all the lot numbers while they waited on the telephone," Estel explained. "They called us twice," she reiterated, "then said they would have a representative in here today (Friday)."

These calls, because of the insistence, appear to have been emergency calls. Kesling Drug received its Tylenol from Zahn Drug's warehouse in Melrose Park. Johnson & Johnson officials were clearly worried about the Extra Strength Tylenol capsules in drugstores that had received shipments from Zahn Drug. The urgent calls from McNeil executives to Kesling were not made out of an overabundance of caution either. Rather, they were targeted emergency calls. Two drugstores several blocks down the road from Kesling Drug—Hook's Drug and Haag Drug—received no such calls from J&J or McNeil. That makes sense, because Hook's Drug and Haag Drug did not receive their Tylenol from Zahn Drug.

Most Chicago-area stores also never received calls or visits like the ones McNeil representatives made to Kesling Drug. A Chicago pharmacist, Robert Wijas, from the Dinet & Delfosse Pharmacy in Chicago, was interviewed by ABC-News six days after the urgent calls from McNeil to Kesling Drug. Wijas said a representative from Johnson & Johnson had been out on Wednesday, October 6th to pick up the pharmacy's inventory of Tylenol capsules. The Dinet & Delfosse Pharmacy was located on North Michigan Avenue in Chicago, just two miles south of the Walgreens store where Paula Prince had purchased a bottle of cyanide-laced Tylenol. Yet no J&J representative visited the Dinet & Delfosse Pharmacy until six days after J&J learned about the Tylenol poisonings. J&J officials were far more concerned about the source of a store's Tylenol than its proximity to Chicago.

The actions of J&J executives indicated that they knew that the Tylenol had been poisoned in the distribution channel. The actions of the Tylenol task force, however, suggested investigators settled on the tampering-in-the-retail-stores theory without conducting a proper investigation of the complex Tylenol manufacturing and distribution network.

On Saturday, October 2nd, Tyrone Fahner said investigators had determined that the tainted capsules did not cross paths while they were being manufactured or in their distribution. He said the cyanide-laced Extra-Strength Tylenol traced to five business locations came from "two and possibly three different places" of distribution. Fahner said that based on what was known, the adulterated capsules from three of the five business locations "definitely did not come together at any time" during distribution. But Fahner didn't have all the facts he needed to determine if the Tylenol capsules had crossed paths.

On October 1st, officials from the Tylenol task force had visited and questioned employees at three Chicago area warehouses: the Certified Grocers warehouse in Hodgkins, the Zahn Drug warehouse in Melrose Park, and the Jewel warehouse in Melrose Park. At this point in the investigation, officials knew that the poisoned Tylenol capsules responsible for deaths of Mary Kellerman and the Januses were purchased at two separate Jewel-Osco stores. Authorities had not yet traced Mary McFarland's Tylenol to the Woolworth store where she bought them, had not yet discovered the body of Paula Prince, and had not revealed the source of Lynn Reiner's cyanide-laced Extra Strength Tylenol capsules.

Investigators visited the Jewel warehouse because they knew that bottles of cyanide-laced Tylenol had been purchased from two Jewel-owned stores. Investigators visited the Certified Grocers warehouse because they knew that Frank's Finer Foods received its Tylenol from the Certified Grocers warehouse and that Lynn Reiner had purchase a bottle of Regular Strength at Frank's Finer Foods. The visit to the Zahn Drug warehouse makes sense only if officials believed that Lynn's Extra Strength Tylenol capsules had come from Central DuPage Hospital and that Central DuPage Hospital received its Tylenol from Zahn Drug.

During an interview with ABC News, Jim Dempsey, the vice president of operations at Zahn Drug, described the scope of the visits by government officials to the company's warehouse. "We've had the Illinois Department of Law Enforcement, we've had the FBI, and we've had the FDA all come in," Dempsey said. "They were principally interested in the lots of Tylenol Extra Strength capsules that we had, and they were also interested in what customers had purchased them, how many, and when."

ABC aired the Dempsey interview on October 6th, but the video footage of the Zahn Drug warehouse shown during that interview had been taken on October 1st, so the interview with Dempsey had evidently been taped back then. By Friday, October 1st, investigators had apparently learned that Lynn Reiner's Extra Strength Tylenol capsules had been dispensed at Central DuPage Hospital and that Central DuPage Hospital received its Tylenol from Zahn Drug.

Johnson & Johnson executives had evidently already identified Zahn Drug as the probable source of the cyanide-laced Extra Strength Tylenol capsules, when, on Thursday morning, September 30th, a McNeil executive phoned Kesling Drug, which received its Tylenol from Zahn Drug, and commanded Estel Kesling to remove all bottles of Extra Strength Tylenol capsules from the store's shelves. At that time, the only two bottles of cyanide-laced Tylenol recovered so far had been purchased at the Jewel-Osco stores in Arlington Heights and Elk Grove Village. J&J executives should have had no reason to suspect that Zahn Drug had delivered cyanide-laced Tylenol capsules to Kesling Drug—unless they knew that Zahn Drug had also distributed bottles of cyanide-laced Tylenol capsules to the Jewel-Osco stores in Elk Grove Village and Arlington Heights.

Zahn Drug was acquired by FoxMeyer in 1989. FoxMeyer went bankrupt in 1996 and McKesson bought the company's remaining assets, which included Zahn Drug. McKesson was the sole supplier of pharmaceuticals to Jewel-Osco stores in the 1990s and received supply management income for purchasing $1.5 billion annually of branded and repackaged pharmaceuticals for Osco Drug warehouses in La Habra, California and Elk Grove Village, Illinois. The five-year distribution agreement between McKesson and Jewel-Osco was renewed in 1998 and again in 2003. Distribution agreements tend to be renewed repeatedly, often for decades, so the genesis of the agreement between McKesson and Jewel may have been an agreement between Jewel Companies and Zahn Drug dating back to before 1982. McKesson is also the current pharmacy service provider for Central DuPage Hospital. Zahn Drug, or a repackager that delivered Tylenol to Zahn Drug, was likely the source of the cyanide-laced Tylenol capsules delivered to Central DuPage Hospital, the Jewel-Osco stores, and all the other Chicago area outlets where cyanide-laced Tylenol was found or purchased.

16

———

The Plot Thickens

On Wednesday, October 6, 1982, one day after Johnson & Johnson initiated the nationwide recall of all Tylenol capsules; the company's head of security brought a letter into the boardroom where the members of J&J's Executive Committee were meeting. The word "TYLENOL" had been handwritten on the letter's envelope. The letter itself said, in part: "If you want the killing to stop, then wire $1 million to #84-49-597 at Continental Illinois Bank in Chicago." That account, closed five months earlier, had belonged to Frederick Miller McCahey, an heir to the Miller Brewing fortune.

Investigators from the FBI and IDLE questioned Frederick McCahey and quickly determined that he had not written the letter. Authorities then asked McCahey to put together a list of names of the individuals who might have a grudge against him. One of the names on that list was Robert Richardson.

Seven days after J&J had received the extortion letter, authorities identified the letter's author as Robert Richardson, aka James Lewis. James and his wife, LeAnn, had lived in Kansas City, Missouri until December 4, 1981 when Kansas City police officers, with a search warrant in hand, showed up on their doorstep. They were investigating James Lewis and George Rea, a former sheriff's deputy, as possible suspects in a credit card fraud scheme. The next day, James and LeAnn left Kansas City. They checked into the Surf Motel in Chicago on December 10, 1981. A week later, using the names Robert and Nancy Richardson, they moved into a rundown West Belden Avenue apartment on Chicago's North Side.

In January 1982, LeAnn got a job at Lakeside Travel, but the company went belly-up just three months later. LeAnn and seventeen other employees were stiffed by the firm's owner, Frederick McCahey, when their final paychecks bounced.

Jim's temporary job at First National Bank of Chicago ended in August 1982. So the Lewises, both now unemployed, packed up their few belongings on September 3rd and took a train to New York City. On September 6th, they rented a room at the Hotel Rutledge on Lexington Avenue and 31st Street in Manhattan.

When the Tylenol murders made front-page news, Lewis saw his chance to draw attention to McCahey and possibly trigger an investigation into what he believed were McCahey's "fraudulent business dealings." Lewis's ill-advised plan involved writing an extortion letter to Johnson & Johnson demanding that the company deposit $1 million into McCahey's business account at Continental Bank.

Tyrone Fahner downplayed the significance of the Tylenol extortion letter. "It will not be relevant in solving the cyanide murders," said Fahner. "It is a whole side issue...a hoax." The FBI eventually arrested Lewis in New York City and charged him with attempted extortion. He was convicted of that crime in October 1983 and sentenced to ten years in prison.

Authorities were still six days away from identifying Lewis as the writer of the Tylenol extortion letter when reports came in on October 7th of two cyanide poisoning deaths that had occurred months earlier in Pennsylvania and Wyoming. Local authorities in Pennsylvania said they had reopened the death investigation of William Pascual, who died in Philadelphia on April 3, 1982 from a cyanide-laced Extra Strength Tylenol capsule. Officials later closed out Pascual's death as a suicide. However, there is substantial evidence that the July cyanide-poisoning death of Jay Mitchell in Wyoming may have been the work of the Tylenol killer.

On Friday, October 8, 1982 a Wyoming FBI agent and a Chicago police detective went to Sheridan, Wyoming, to help local authorities determine whether the death of Jay Adam Mitchell was linked to the Tylenol murders in Illinois. Mitchell, a 19-year-old school janitor from the town of Big Horn, had failed to turn off his alarm clock when it went off at 6:30 a.m., July 26, 1982. His father tried to wake him, but Mitchell was dead. An older brother told the

Chicago detective that he thought Mitchell took Tylenol from a bottle in the kitchen four hours before his alarm went off. Mitchell's mother also said he had taken Extra Strength Tylenol shortly before his death.

Sheridan County Coroner Jim Kane said the Tylenol capsules were not suspected until after Mitchell's toxicology test results came back from Utah, three weeks before the Tylenol murders. By then, Mrs. Mitchell had thrown out the Tylenol bottle.

Dr. William Doughty, a pathologist at the Sheridan County Memorial Hospital who was familiar with the case, became suspicious about Mitchell's death after hearing news of the deaths from cyanide-filled Tylenol capsules in Illinois. Dr. Doughty asked Mrs. Mitchell if her son had taken any medication before his death. According to Doughty, she replied, "Nothing, just a headache pill; some Extra-Strength Tylenol." He also said, "She said she thought she had purchased it at Buttrey-Osco, a local food and drug store."

Doughty asked the manager at the local Buttrey-Osco store where the Extra Strength Tylenol came from and was told that since March 1982 the store has purchased its Tylenol from the Jewel Tea Company of Chicago—aka Jewel Companies, Inc. of Melrose Park, Illinois. The Buttrey-Osco stores were part of Jewel's Osco Drug subsidiary. Cyanide-laced Tylenol capsules had now been linked to four Jewel Companies stores—the Buttrey-Osco store in Sheridan, the Jewel-Osco stores in Elk Grove Village and Arlington Heights, and the Osco Drug store in Schaumburg.

A second analysis of the contents of Mitchell's stomach, conducted the first week of October 1982, revealed the exact same dosage of cyanide as was found in the stomach contents of the Chicago victims. Dr. Bryan Finkle, the director of the Center for Human Toxicology at the University of Utah, compared the Wyoming death with the deaths in Illinois. "It turned out," said Dr. Finkle, "that there were a lot of similarities toxicologically" with the Mitchell case and the poisoning cases in Illinois. "It was exactly the same as the Mitchell dosage," explained Dr. Finkle. "It's a very tight link. It would be very difficult for these different people to take exactly the same dosage of cyanide without having taken the same-sized capsule with the same-sized dosage."

The evidence "as it stands in no way makes a case," remarked Dr. Finkle, but he also felt that considerable further research was necessary in this case and others. "If the deaths were not clustered, there is every reason to believe they would all have been signed out as cyanide deaths [not linked to Tylenol capsules] and there would have been no connection made, meaning the method, modus operandi."

Officials never found the source of the cyanide that killed Mitchell—or if they did, they never disclosed that source. When the Chicago detective returned home from Wyoming on Sunday, October 10th, Chicago Police Sergeant Michael Invergo announced that investigators had turned up nothing new after traveling to Sheridan. Authorities dismissed the similarities between the poisonings in Wyoming and Illinois, declaring them unrelated. In so doing, they had ignored an awful lot of evidence, as well as the advice of Dr. Finkle.

*****

In addition to the cyanide deaths linked to Tylenol capsules in Wyoming and Philadelphia, there were also other cyanide poisoning deaths in Cook County around the time of the Tylenol murders. Robert Stein announced on October 1, 1982 that the Cook County Medical Examiner's Office had begun to review all sudden unexplained deaths that had occurred after September 1, 1982. Stein said they were re-testing frozen blood samples from recent unexplained deaths in Cook County in cases where the victim had died suddenly and initial autopsy results showed the presence of Tylenol in the bloodstream.

Stein's decision to use Tylenol (acetaminophen) as a qualifier for determining whether blood samples should be re-tested makes it clear that autopsies conducted in Cook County routinely tested for acetaminophen. That makes sense, as hundreds of deaths each year are caused by accidental and intentional acetaminophen poisoning. Acetaminophen is second only to alcohol as the most common drug involved in suicides from drug overdoses.

On January 13, 1983, Robert Stein said his office had reviewed the autopsy results from 17 unexplained deaths in Cook County.

The medical examiners found that three of these deaths were from cyanide poisoning. Autopsies conducted in Cook and DuPage Counties did not routinely screen for the presence of cyanide, so the examiners in Cook County had initially misclassified, rather innocently, the cause of death for these three individuals.

"We are continuing these investigations [into other unexplained deaths] because we are finding now that cyanide is an easy poison to obtain," Stein explained, "and we don't want to overlook any possible cyanide poisoning case."

The three reopened death investigations in Cook County came about because toxicologists had retested the blood samples recently taken from individuals suspected to have overdosed on cocaine and found that they had actually died from cyanide poisoning. Michael Schaffer, the Cook County Chief Toxicologist, said officials were checking the deaths of Mark Husted, age 32, originally from West Dundee, IL; Galen Parriott, age 30, of Skokie, IL; and Marie Louise Watkins, age 21, of Chicago, "because of the close proximity [in time] to the cyanide deaths [of the Tylenol murders victims]."

Husted had died Tuesday, September 14th, two weeks before the Tylenol murders; Watkins had died on August 15th, six weeks before the Tylenol murders; and Parriott died on December 1st, two months after the murders. Cook County medical examiners found acetaminophen and lethal levels of cyanide in the blood samples taken from all three victims.

An un-named detective on the Tylenol task force said it would be valuable information to know if the cyanide that caused these three deaths was the same type that had killed the Tylenol victims, but he said it was impossible to conduct such a test.

When Cook County medical examiners had conducted an autopsy on Mary Watkins, they had found only traces of metabolized cocaine in her body. They had ruled her death a cocaine overdose nonetheless. Upon retesting Watkins's blood samples in October, authorities determined that cyanide, not cocaine, had caused her death. Toxicology tests found both cyanide and acetaminophen in her body. Yet Jaye Schroeder, a Chicago police spokesperson, said on October 27th that the Tylenol task force was not investigating Watkins's death because it was not clear whether her death was a homicide.

Dr. Mitra Kalelkar, the assistant medical examiner for Cook County who had examined Watkins's remains, said, "We cannot definitely find a link between the other Tylenol cyanide cases and this case because we have not determined the source of the cyanide." Kalelkar said she and her associates had not determined conclusively that there was no connection between the cyanide-poisoning death of Watkins and those of the seven victims officially linked to the Tylenol murders. "Anything is possible," she said.

*****

The Mark Husted cyanide poisoning case is also interesting. Husted was a convicted drug dealer who was to appear in the U.S. District Court in Chicago on November 8, 1982 on charges of conspiring to sell cocaine. Husted and one of his friends, Louis Tedesco, had been charged in a 79-count indictment, along with thirteen others, for their involvement in a cocaine smuggling operation.

Husted had flown to Chicago O'Hare International Airport from his home in Florida on Tuesday, September 14, 1982. He then drove to Louis Tedesco's house on Anita Street in Des Plaines, Illinois. Husted was expected the next day at his parent's home in West Dundee, Illinois, but he died Tuesday night. Tedesco told police that he found Husted slumped over on the back porch and then called the paramedics.

Agents from the Drug Enforcement Administration (DEA) reported on September 16th that Husted's death was believed to have been caused by a drug overdose, but they said the autopsy conducted on September 15th was inconclusive. It was only because Mark's father, Richard Husted, asked authorities to reopen the investigation of his son's death that medical examiners went back and re-tested Mark's blood and tissue samples for cyanide. Richard Husted, who had been a state's attorney in Greene County, Illinois in the 1950s, urged the re-investigation because of "a feeling that his son may have been murdered."

The second set of toxicology tests showed lethal levels of cyanide in Mark Husted's body tissues. Results from these tests were known shortly before the Tylenol murders case broke, but they were not made public until January 13, 1983. Officials delayed publicizing the coroner's findings for ten weeks, possibly to keep Husted's case separate from the Tylenol murders.

Members of Mark Husted's family said he had been mixed up with a Colombian drug cartel. He was facing a potentially long prison term for his alleged involvement in a drug smuggling operation. However, if someone related to drugs had wanted to murder Husted, they would probably not have used cyanide. Authorities never found the source of the cyanide that killed Husted.

Was Mark Husted murdered to keep him from talking—or was he another victim of the Tylenol killer? Husted had a habit that suggests the latter. Family members said he "ate Tylenol like it was candy."

Some of the Tylenol killer's cyanide-laced Tylenol capsules may have already been bottled and distributed to Chicago-area stores when Mark Husted flew into O'Hare International Airport on September 14th. From that airport, Husted had driven to Tedesco's house in Des Plaines, passing the exits to the Osco Drug store in Schaumburg and the Jewel-Osco store in Elk Grove Village where bottles of cyanide-laced Tylenol capsules were found or purchased two weeks later. Maybe Husted stopped at a local supermarket or drugstore to pick up a bottle of Extra Strength Tylenol capsules on the way to Tedesco's house.

Cook County medical examiners found cyanide and acetaminophen in the blood or body tissues of cyanide-poisoning victims Mark Husted, Mary Watkins, and Galen Parriott. In addition, Jay Mitchell had died of cyanide poisoning in Wyoming shortly after taking Extra Strength Tylenol capsules purchased from a store in Sheridan that received its Tylenol from the same Illinois warehouse that distributed Tylenol to the Jewel-Osco stores in the Chicago area. The official Tylenol murders death toll is seven, but there is no evidence to exclude any of these four individuals as additional victims of the Tylenol killer.

17

A Poisoned Investigation

By October 9, 1982, Cook County Medical Examiner Dr. Robert Stein had been monitoring, for nine days, the "test capsules" that he and his staff had filled with cyanide to determine its corrosive effects on the Tylenol capsules. Authorities claimed that the cyanide used by the Tylenol killer was highly corrosive and would have eaten through the gelatin-based Tylenol capsules very quickly; thus, according to Illinois Attorney General Tyrone Fahner, the tamperings must have occurred at the local retail stores, probably on Tuesday, the day before the murders.

The evidence does support the assertion of officials who said cyanide would cause the gel-based shells of the Tylenol capsules to corrode (the water in cyanide, not the cyanide itself, actually causes the capsules to corrode). However, the evidence discredits their assertion that the cyanide-laced capsules would show visible signs of corrosion in just two days.

Cook County Toxicologist Michael Schaffer said the cyanide from the poisoned capsules in the Kellerman and Janus bottles was moist and had caused the capsules to corrode. Those capsules, when inspected one day after the poisonings, were somewhat swollen and discolored. The one remaining cyanide-laced capsule in Paula Prince's Tylenol bottle, inspected two days after the murders, was also discolored and swollen.

On October 21, 1982, a J&J employee working at the company's temporary lab in Lemont discovered another bottle of cyanide-laced Extra Strength Tylenol capsules. That bottle, the seventh bottle of cyanide-laced Tylenol, bore the lot number MC2880, which was also the lot number on Mary Kellerman's and the Januses' Tylenol bottles. The seventh bottle had been returned to a Dominick's supermarket store in Chicago on October 3rd, but it had not been purchased there. The person who turned it in was never found. Fahner said the cyanide-laced capsules in the seventh bottle, inspected 22 days after the murders, were in an "advanced state of deterioration." They had corroded to a much greater degree than the cyanide-laced Tylenol capsules Schaffer had inspected about three weeks earlier.

The cyanide-laced Extra Strength Tylenol capsules recovered after the April 1982 poisoning death of William Pascual provided another example of the corrosive effects of moist cyanide. When those capsules were first discovered, they showed no signs of corrosion. But when re-examined on October 9, 1982, they had degraded into nothing but powder—the result of extensive corrosion in the preceding six months caused by the moist cyanide.

To find out when and where the Tylenol tamperings occurred, authorities first needed to figure out how long it had taken the cyanide-laced Tylenol capsules to show signs of degradation. This is exactly what Robert Stein had set out to do on the morning of Thursday, September 30th when he and his staff "duplicated" the victims' cyanide-laced Tylenol capsules. Stein then monitored these test capsules to determine how long it would take for them to show signs of corrosion. Officials from J&J and the Tylenol task force never talked about this forensic analysis. But Robert Stein did talk. He said that after the cyanide had been in the test capsules for 48 hours, they still showed no signs of corrosion.

On October 9th, Stein said that he had completed tests indicating that the cyanide-loaded Tylenol capsules could have been doctored at their distribution points or at the plant where they were produced. At this point, ten days after the test capsules had been filled with cyanide, they still did not show (or had just begun to show) visible signs of corrosion.

Tyrone Fahner reacted to Stein's findings by sharply criticizing Stein for suggesting that the Tylenol capsules had been poisoned at the manufacturing plant or in the distribution channel. Stein's findings were never mentioned publicly again.

Even James Lewis questioned the failure of authorities to produce clear evidence related to the corrosive capability of cyanide on the Tylenol capsules. In a 1992 prison interview with ABC News, Lewis, convicted nine years earlier for attempted extortion, said, "The Illinois Department of Law Enforcement, the FBI— apparently none of those [agencies] ever did a shelf-life test [on the cyanide-laced Tylenol capsules]. I have long contended that if you find the person who squelched the shelf-life test, you will be very close to the person who committed the Tylenol murders." Lewis believed that one or more individuals had suppressed information that should have been used to help investigators track down the Tylenol killer.

The cyanide in the adulterated Tylenol capsules did indeed cause the capsules to corrode, but not in just one to a few days as was suggested by every official who spoke publicly about the case, other than Robert Stein. Some or all of the cyanide-laced Tylenol capsules in the Kellerman, Janus, and Prince bottles showed visible signs of corrosion one to two days after the murders, and thus had been filled with cyanide about ten days or more before they were purchased on September 28th and 29th. However, not all of the cyanide-laced Tylenol capsules showed signs of corrosion.

On October 8, 1982, NBC News aired video footage taken at the Illinois Department of Health lab in DuPage County. The video showed the four cyanide-laced red and white Extra Strength Tylenol capsules that had been in Lynn Reiner's bottle of gray and white Regular Strength Tylenol capsules. Extreme close-up shots revealed that none of these cyanide-laced capsules had any visible signs of corrosion. They were in perfect condition, with no discoloration or swelling, and thus had been filled with cyanide more recently than the cyanide-laced Tylenol capsules from the Kellerman, Janus, and Prince bottles.

Tyrone Fahner said the cyanide-laced Tylenol capsules from the different bottles looked different. He said the tampering for some capsules could be detected "by the naked eye," but others showed no visible evidence that they had been opened and their contents switched.

The Tylenol capsules that could be detected by the naked eye as having visible signs of corrosion had been filled with cyanide more than ten days before the murders. The Tylenol capsules with no visible signs of tampering had been filled with cyanide more recently.

The FDA, using an analytical tool developed by Ames Laboratory, traced the cyanide that was used by the Tylenol killer to DuPont. The chemical make-up of the cyanide in all of the victims' Tylenol capsules was identical. The varying degrees of corrosion on different capsules were thus not a function of dissimilar chemical makeup. The *Chicago Tribune* reported that the poisoned Tylenol capsules contained three different mixes of cyanide, but they differed only in the fineness to which the crystals were ground.

Robert Stein's shelf life tests soundly debunked the claim made by officials who cited the super-corrosiveness of cyanide as their only evidence that the tamperings had occurred in the retail stores one day before the Tylenol murders. In early 1986, the FDA conducted its own analysis of cyanide-laced Tylenol capsules at the agency's most sophisticated lab for analyzing poisons. This analysis was done on Tylenol capsules containing cyanide with "low water content." The FDA found that these cyanide-laced capsules would show no signs of degradation for many months. The degraded condition of some of the cyanide-laced Tylenol capsules further indicated they had been poisoned within the Tylenol manufacturing and distribution network, before they were delivered the retail stores.

18

A Shelf-life Problem

The Tylenol monograph states that under room temperature storage conditions, Tylenol acetaminophen solid formulations are generally stable for three years from the date of manufacture for commercially available products. The source of the stability data for this three-year shelf life is a 1974 study: Fairbrother, J. "Acetaminophen." New York, NY: Academic Press; 1974.

Dean Mickelson, a pharmacist at the Revco drugstore in Taos, New Mexico, referenced the three-year shelf life of Tylenol during an interview with a reporter from *The Taos News*. Mickelson told *The Taos News* on October 6, 1982 that Tylenol had a shelf life to 1985, meaning the Tylenol manufactured in 1982 would expire three years later, in 1985.

Forty months later, Jack Ogun, the director of the Division of Drugs, Devices, and Cosmetics for the Pennsylvania State Health Department, also referenced the three-year shelf life of Tylenol. Ogun said the May 1987 expiration date of a tainted bottle of Tylenol discovered in February 1986 indicated it would have been in stores for about two years because non-prescription pain-relievers generally have a shelf life of about three years.

Oddly, all of the Tylenol involved in the 1982 Tylenol murders had a shelf life of *five* years—two years longer than the three-year shelf life described in the Tylenol monograph. This five-year shelf life was never mentioned by J&J executives or government officials. The press briefly publicized the expiration dates for only Lots MC2880 and 1910MD.

Close-up photographs of Tylenol bottles bearing lot numbers MC2880 and 1910MD ran in many newspapers, and the expiration dates in these photos were clearly visible. The Tylenol from Lot

MC2880 was in the Janus and Kellerman bottles, and had an expiration date of April 1987. The Tylenol from Lot 1910MD was in Mary McFarland's bottle, and had an expiration date of May 1987. The expiration date of Lynn Reiner's cyanide-laced Tylenol is unknown, but the Tylenol involved in all the other murders had expiration dates of between February 1987 and May 1987, and was manufactured between January and May of 1982.

An FOIA request was filed with the FDA in June 2011 seeking documents describing the expiration dating of Tylenol produced in McNeil's manufacturing plants in 1982. The FDA responded, stating: "Tylenol and other acetaminophen products are marketed and labeled under the OTC drug monograph and without an approved application housing such records."

The FDA did not produce the requested information, but it did confirm that the Tylenol expiration dating is based on the Tylenol monograph, which uses stability data from a 1974 study to set the shelf-life of Tylenol at three years. In 1982, Tylenol typically had a shelf life of three years—with the notable exception of the Tylenol that Johnson & Johnson sold to the United States Department of Defense (DOD).

In 1973, the DOD had sought to defer drug replacement costs for date sensitive stockpiles of prescription and OTC drugs by extending their useful life beyond the manufacturer's original expiration date. Subsequently, the Office of Management and Budget and the General Accounting Office completed studies to determine the feasibility of a "shelf life extension program." These agencies found that the shelf life of OTC drugs, generally two to three years, could safely be extended to five years under properly controlled storage conditions.

On July 1, 1975, the FDA and the Veterans Administration (VA) entered into a "Memo of Understanding" implementing a program to extend the expiration dates to five years for prescription and OTC drugs sold to all branches of the DOD. The FDA was charged with monitoring this program, which applied only to drugs purchased by the DOD for use in military facilities and for sale in military commissaries.

Throughout the 1980s, the DOD purchased Tylenol in bulk containers for use in military treatment facilities, VA hospitals, and clinics. The DOD also purchased Tylenol for retail sale in its military commissaries. Because of the shelf-life extension program, all the Tylenol sold to the DOD was given a shelf life of five years. This extended-expiration-dating required separate bottling production runs so the labels on the Tylenol bottles sold to the DOD reflected the five-year shelf life rather than the typical three-year shelf life of the Tylenol that was bottled at the McNeil manufacturing plants.

At the time of the Tylenol murders, military commissaries were indeed selling bottles of Extra Strength Tylenol capsules from the lots involved in the poisonings. On Friday, October 1, 1982, state officials in Kansas said at least 180 bottles of Tylenol from the contaminated lots were found at Fort Riley. A Fort Riley spokesperson, Milt Sheeley, said Tylenol capsules were removed from the commissary and other shops that day. "We're yanking it. We're advising everybody to throw the capsules away," said Sheeley.

Public Affairs Officer Jane Wray said the manager of the Fort Leavenworth commissary found "a number of bottles" of Tylenol from the recalled lot, 1910MD.

Air Force officials also discovered several cases of Extra Strength Tylenol capsules with recalled lot numbers at the Chanute Air Force Base in Illinois and at the Lakeland Air Force Base in San Antonio, Texas. Air Force officials said the Tylenol from the suspect lots were turned over to civilian authorities.

Some of the Tylenol purchased in 1982 by the DOD and sold in military commissaries may have been diverted for civilian retail sale. Drug diversion was a big problem in the 1980s and the subject of several Congressional hearings. Diverters actively sought out hospitals, long-term-care pharmacies, and Federal Supply Schedule (FSS) purchasers that bought drugs at discounted prices not available to wholesalers in the retail class of trade. The diverters then sold these discounted drugs for a quick profit to wholesalers.

According to a March 19, 1982 GAO report, military commissary procurement divisions conducted a substantial amount of business through independent vendors, whose representatives performed in-store services, such as merchandising, reordering, and inventory stocking. In other words, the representatives who handled the ordering and restocking of Tylenol at the DOD commissaries were rack jobbers and merchandisers like the ones employed in the Chicago area by Sav-A-Stop and Zahn Drug.

A Chicago area third-party distributor that delivered Tylenol to the DOD Supply Depot in Hines (four miles south of Zahn Drug), and to Chicago area military commissaries, may have been the same distributor that shipped cyanide-laced Extra Strength Tylenol capsules to Chicago-area outlets in September 1982. If the Tylenol killer put cyanide-laced Tylenol capsules into the bottling production lines at a repackaging facility under contract with Johnson & Johnson to bottle Tylenol for the United States Department of Defense, then the federal government had motive to suppress that information and keep secret its inability to secure the Military's drug supply system.

Spokespersons for J&J and the FDA never succinctly described the true manufacturing, packaging, or distribution process of the Tylenol found poisoned in the Chicago area. They said Tylenol was packaged at the "factory," but they never said the Tylenol from the poisoned lots had been packaged at the *McNeil* factory. J&J spokespersons said the first batch of Tylenol implicated in the poisonings had been shipped to a warehouse in Franklin Park between the 19th and 25th of August 1982, but they never identified the owner of that warehouse.

J&J spokesperson Marshall Molloy said that McNeil supplied Extra Strength Tylenol from plants in both Round Rock and Fort Washington to "100 or so" wholesale distributors in the Chicago area market. But McNeil did not ship Tylenol to those 100 or so wholesalers directly from the McNeil manufacturing plants. The Tylenol was instead shipped to the Illinois wholesalers from J&J's regional distribution center in Montgomeryville, Pennsylvania, which was really much more than just a distribution center. It was the headquarters of the R. W. Johnson Pharmaceutical Research Institute, McNeil Labs, and the McNeil Pharmaceutical Company. And it also housed one of two McNeil Pharmaceutical manufacturing plants.

Large fiber drums containing Tylenol powder were regularly shipped to J&J's Montgomeryville facility in 1982 and used by the McNeil Pharmaceutical Company to manufacture Tylox capsules, a prescription painkiller containing a combination of Tylenol and the narcotic oxycodone. Some containers of bulk Tylenol may have been shipped from J&J's Montgomeryville facility to a repackaging facility in the Chicago area where the tamperings actually occurred.

To solve the Tylenol murders, officials needed to trace all of the cyanide-laced Tylenol capsules back to the central repackaging facility where they had been handled. Officials instead jumped to the conclusion that the Tylenol killer had put the cyanide-laced Tylenol capsules into Tylenol bottles *after* the bottles were shipped to the retail stores. They agreed to turn over the Chicago-area Tylenol capsules to Johnson & Johnson on the first day of the investigation, and they set out to build a case against the man they had targeted early in the investigation as the prime suspect for the Tylenol murders.

19

———

We Know Who Did It

During the first four days of the Tylenol murders investigation, the Tylenol task force interviewed about 1,000 people and developed a list of about 24 suspects. On Tuesday, October 5th, the sixth day of the investigation, Tyrone Fahner said the suspect list had been reduced to "eight or nine" prime suspects. He said they were all Illinois residents, and some had a history of mental illness. "All were available to the location, exhibited peculiar behavior, or had a grudge as a possible motive," Fahner revealed. "They are not being sought," he said. "We know who they are." Fahner said all were under surveillance around the clock, and at least two had been interviewed. Asked if the others were aware of their police tails, Fahner replied, "I hope not."

One day later, Fanner said that "the list of suspects has been narrowed," but he refused to specify by how many. "I've been advised by investigators not to play a numbers game," he explained.

On October 9th, Fahner, anxious to convey some level of progress in the case, was back in the numbers game again. He now said investigators had cut their list of eight or nine suspects to "four main suspects." Two had been interviewed, and some were under constant surveillance. By the end of that same day, authorities eliminated another suspect, leaving only three main suspects. Fahner said six prime suspects had been eliminated because they had recently passed lie detector tests.

Jerome Howard, the man removed from Fahner's suspect list on October 9th, had left a letter on a receptionist's desk at Gottlieb Memorial Hospital in Melrose Park on Thursday, October 7th warning that patients would be poisoned with cyanide-laced Extra-Strength Tylenol unless a package containing $8,000 was left near the hospital's maternity ward. The letter read, "Me and my gang put cyanide in every bottle of Extra-Strength Tylenol to see what it will do...Like seven deaths isn't funny, but eight more will be."

Howard, a 20-year-old former employee of Gottlieb Memorial Hospital, was picked up on October 8th near the hospital's maternity ward when he attempted to retrieve the ransom packet. A joint statement released by Tyrone Fahner and Edward Hegarty, the special agent in charge of the FBI's Chicago office, said, "There is no credible evidence to indicate directly or indirectly" that Howard played any role in the poisonings. Fahner said the Howard case was unrelated totally to the Tylenol deaths, though he did admit Howard once had been one of their main suspects.

Two of the remaining three names on Fahner's whittled down list of prime suspects belonged to relatives of the Tylenol murders victims. The Tylenol task force had zeroed in specifically on the relatives of Lynn Reiner. The investigative strategy in the Reiner murder case was revealed in a news report on October 8, 1982, when James Polk, reporting in Chicago for NBC *Nightly News*, said, "Police believe the poisoned capsules [that killed Lynn Reiner] were placed in the Frank's Finer Food store in Winfield on Wednesday [September 29, 1982]."

"This is the case that does not fit the pattern," said Polk. "Winfield is a village 30 miles from downtown Chicago, and even the food store is hard to find. Lynn Reiner came here [to Frank's Finer Foods] at 3 p.m. that day – as usual, she bought Regular Strength Tylenol. At home, Mrs. Reiner took one of these capsules (video showing Lynn's Tylenol capsules being handled by a lab worker at the Illinois Department of Health in Wheaton) and it killed her. Mixed in with these gray Regular Strength capsules were red and white Extra Strength capsules—five laced with cyanide."

Polk then added, "Investigators think Winfield may not have been chosen at random—that someone in a deliberate effort came here to make the switch at Frank's Finer Foods."

Investigators were evidently working under the assumption that the Tylenol killer had targeted Lynn Reiner specifically. The NBC report provided a clue that investigators may also have been working on the hypothesis that the killer might have planted cyanide-laced capsules at Central DuPage Hospital. NBC reported that Frank's Finer Foods "is directly across the street from the entrance to Central DuPage Hospital. The FBI has asked for the record of all patients who have been through the psychiatric ward here."

When investigators determined that the Tylenol killer could not have planted poisoned Tylenol capsules at the closed-door pharmacy at Central DuPage Hospital, they came up with a scenario of how the killer could have put the cyanide-laced Extra Strength capsules into a bottle of Regular Strength Tylenol at Frank's Finer Foods. This was a story that prosecutors could use to explain how eight red and white Extra Strength Tylenol capsules (five laced with cyanide) had gotten into Lynn's bottle of gray and white Regular Strength Tylenol capsules.

Lynn Reiner did buy a bottle of Regular Strength Tylenol at Frank's Finer Foods, but the bottle did not contain any cyanide-laced capsules when she bought it. When Lynn returned home with her new bottle of Regular Strength Tylenol, she found the unit-dose package of eight Extra Strength Tylenol capsules that she'd been given at the hospital. She swallowed two of those Extra Strength capsules—one filled with cyanide—and put the other six into her Regular Strength Tylenol bottle. She then tossed the empty unit-dose package, along with the box for the Regular Strength Tylenol, into the trash can below her kitchen sink. At the time, only Lynn Reiner knew about the unit-dose package of Extra Strength Tylenol capsules.

The Winfield police would not confirm or deny whether they recovered the unit-dose package for Lynn's Extra Strength Tylenol capsules. However, on March 9, 2010, Scott Watkins, the Winfield police officer primarily responsible for the investigation of Lynn's murder, told Lynn's daughter, Michelle, that they had indeed found the box for Lynn's bottle of Regular Strength Tylenol capsules in the trash can at Reiner's home on September 30, 1982. They likely also found the unit-dose package bearing the lot number 1665LM and the name "Central DuPage Hospital" in the same trash can. Investigators did not tell Lynn's relatives about what they had found, because some of them were already suspects.

On October 9, 1982, an unidentified member of the Tylenol task force told reporters for *USA Today* that authorities knew who committed the Tylenol murders. The source said investigators had targeted a Chicago-area man as the prime suspect. "We know who did it. We just have to prove it," he said. "If this guy doesn't work out, we're pretty much down to the end of the rope."

Based on this statement from the *USA Today* source, and on the NBC News report from the previous day, it looked like one of Lynn's relatives was about to be arrested and charged for the Tylenol murders. But then, a man who called himself a "closet chemist" entered the picture and muddled everything up.

20

The Closet Chemist

On Saturday evening, October 9, 1982, Roger Arnold, a 48-year-old, wiry, chain-smoking warehouse worker, stopped off for a few drinks at O'Rourke's Tavern, an Irish pub located in Lincoln Park on Chicago's North Side. Arnold entered the tavern carrying a plastic bag of white powder that he said was cyanide. He then allegedly made comments about killing people with cyanide. The tavern's owner, Marty Sinclair, picked up the phone and called the Chicago Police. He told them Arnold was a peculiar bird who kept test-tubes, guns, and two vials of cyanide in his house.

Two days later, Arnold was in Lilly's Bar, down the street from O'Rourke's Tavern, when Chicago police detectives entered the bar and picked-up Arnold on an outstanding arrest warrant for aggravated assault. With Arnold's permission, the police searched his house on Chicago's south side. They confiscated one bolt-action rifle, four handguns, and a stockpile of ammunition.

Chicago police arrested Arnold and charged him with failing to register the weapons and on the prior charge of aggravated assault. Arnold was held without bail so he could be questioned about the Tylenol murders. Arnold later said authorities had handcuffed him to a chair and interrogated him Monday night, October 11th, and again on Tuesday.

Roger Arnold, born on July 29, 1934, was adopted by Mable and Walter Arnold of Chicago in September 1934. Mable was a stay-at-home mom. Walter was a supervisor for Butler Brothers, Inc. Arnold grew up in an apartment in Pearl Court in Chicago. He dropped out of school in the seventh grade and then worked various jobs. At age 18, he got a job working at the Kemper Insurance warehouse in Chicago and moved out of his parents' home. Arnold entered the Army in 1957 and eventually achieved the rank of corporal. He was discharged from the Army in 1959 and resumed his job at the Kemper Insurance warehouse.

In 1969, Arnold took a job as a warehouse worker for Jewel Companies and was still employed there when he became a suspect in the Tylenol murders case. Arnold was a foreman and union steward in Jewel's salvage operation at the company's Melrose Park distribution facility.

Prior to the aggravated assault charge in June 1982, and his arrest in the Tylenol case in October, Arnold had a couple other brushes with the law. Arnold had been arrested in Chicago in 1968 for aggravated assault and unlawful use of a weapon. The charges were later dismissed. In 1981, Arnold was arrested in DuPage County and charged with possession of marijuana. He was found not guilty.

Of special interest to Chicago police was that Arnold had recently stored cyanide in his basement and had used it for unspecified "projects." Arnold said he had purchased the cyanide "some months ago" but then discarded it in August of 1982—the same month that the Tylenol from some or all of the lots linked to the poisonings were shipped to Illinois.

Chicago Police Detective James Gildea said Arnold called himself a "closet chemist." According to Gildea, Arnold had a working knowledge of chemicals and compounds.

On Tuesday afternoon, Chicago Police Detectives, Donald Eddy and Robert Rebholz, both members of the Tylenol task force, arrived at precinct headquarters on Chicago's North Side at 4:00 p.m. They spent an hour and-a-half sifting through a stack of worthless tips from conspiracy theorists and psychics before Lieutenant August Locallo asked them to follow up on a lead. "You can read whatever you want into this," remarked Locallo, "but there are a lot of suspicious coincidences" surrounding Arnold. Locallo said Arnold had cyanide in his house and he worked at Jewel, the company where the father (Howard Fearon, Sr.) of one of the victims (Lynn Reiner) worked as a truck driver.

Jewel, with more than 55,000 employees was one of the largest employers in Illinois. It operated huge warehouses, distribution centers, and packaging plants in Melrose Park, Franklin Park, Elk Grove Village, Barrington, and several other towns in suburban Chicago. Fearon and Arnold did not actually work together. They didn't even know each other.

"At first [Arnold] denied that he had any cyanide," remarked Locallo, "and then admitted that he did have some cyanide…but got rid of it." Arnold said he had previously kept cyanide in his basement for "experiments," added Locallo. "[Arnold] dropped the comment that he's interested in catching the killer of this Tylenol case," said Locallo, "that a friend of his is a truck spotter at the Jewel parking lot, and this friend of his daughter was the one (Lynn Reiner) that died in the Winfield incident."

Locallo said they had received a tip that Arnold's former wife had been hospitalized at the psychiatric ward at Central DuPage Hospital. "I want you to check out [Arnold's] ex-wife and see what she knows."

The detectives took a squad car and headed toward the North Side home of Arnold's ex-wife, Delores Keas. A few minutes later they turned onto North Monticello Avenue and pulled into Delores's driveway. She lived in the house with her 74-year-old brother. Delores invited the detectives into her cluttered living room where they casually interviewed her for more than an hour.

Arnold had married Delores in 1970, and they had moved into an apartment in Forrest Park, a Western suburb of Chicago. In 1981 they bought a house in nearby Oakbrook Terrace, but Arnold moved out the following year when Delores filed for divorce. The divorce was finalized in July 1982.

Delores could not believe her ex-husband was "goofy enough" to get involved in anything like the Tylenol killings. She said her husband had become interested in chemistry about six months ago, and chemicals were delivered to the house in Oakbrook Terrace. She said on one occasion, a number of years ago, Arnold had given her a Tylenol pill and she vomited, but that "was probably due to overeating," she clarified.

Detectives Eddy and Rebholz finished questioning Delores and then took a break for dinner. On the way back to headquarters, they received a call from dispatch with instructions to head down to

Chicago's South Side to stake out Roger Arnold's house on the corner of South Hoyne Avenue and 34th Street.

For nearly two hours, Eddy and Rebholz sat in their car and watched Arnold's small brown house. Finally, at about 11 p.m., five police cars pulled up. A team of investigators from the forensic laboratory had a search warrant for Arnold's residence. Chicago police had searched the house on Monday night, but now investigators went inside with vacuum cleaners to conduct a second, more thorough search. Warrants had also been granted to search Arnold's car and work locker at Jewel. Eddy and Rebholz drove back to the North Side to keep an eye on Arnold's red Chevrolet, which was parked on a street under the "L" train tracks. A forensic team arrived a few minutes before 1 a.m. to search the vehicle.

While searching Arnold's house, investigators found two one-way tickets to Thailand. They confiscated a number of books and magazines, including a stash of *Soldier of Fortune* magazines, *The Anarchist Cookbook* of "recipes" for making explosive devices, and *The Poor Man's James Bond*, a handbook written by right-wing survivalist and former minuteman Kurt Saxon (a.k.a. Donald Sisco). Police confiscated several training manuals published in the mid-1960s by the United States Department of Defense for use by U.S. Army Special Forces. These training manuals included *Incendiaries*, *Boobytraps*, *Unconventional Warfare Devices & Techniques*, and *Military Chemistry & Chemical Agents*. Police found lab equipment and various chemicals, including large quantities of a particular type of hair gel used in some of the bomb-making recipes found in *The Anarchist Cookbook*.

Police also turned up a suspicious-looking plastic bag of white powder, and a book with instructions for encapsulating cyanide. The white powder was turned over to the Chicago Health Department laboratory. A spokesperson for the Chicago police later said a lab test found that the powder was a harmless carbonate.

Arnold was held without bond while city detectives followed up on the circumstantial evidence that led them to consider him a possible suspect in the Tylenol poisonings. Lieutenant Locallo said a series of coincidences had surfaced when Arnold talked with investigators, and they had no choice but to investigate further. The press reported these coincidences were that Arnold told police he had kept cyanide at his house until August; that he had allegedly threatened to kill his estranged wife with cyanide capsules; he worked at a warehouse that officials said was a distribution point for some of the poisoned Tylenol; and he worked with the father of one of the Tylenol victims.

Furthermore, Marty Sinclair was not the only tavern owner who heard Arnold talk about poisoning people with cyanide. According to the *Daily Herald*, Arnold reportedly told *several* Chicago tavern owners rambling stories about killing people with cyanide

Arnold was released from jail on Wednesday night, October 13th after paying $600 to a bondsman who then posted the $6,000 bail bond: $1,000 for each of the unregistered gun charges, and another $1,000 for the charge of aggravated assault.

The assault charge stemmed from a June 1982 incident when Arnold, during a violent argument with Marty Sinclair, pointed a gun at Sinclair. Chicago Police Detective Jerry Beam said Sinclair had provided police with the tip that led to Arnold's arrest as a suspect in the Tylenol murders case.

Detective Marty Ryan confirmed that police had arrested Arnold because of a tip that he had two bottles of cyanide, but he said none of that poison was found in his South Side home. "It doesn't appear [that Arnold] is linked with the Tylenol poisonings," said Ryan. Nevertheless, Chicago police immediately put Arnold under around-the-clock surveillance.

Arnold's lawyer, Thomas Royce, a well-known Chicago defense attorney, later said that the police scrutiny was relentless and continued for weeks. Royce said the surveillance was so heavy that he and Arnold began meeting in McKinley Park, near Arnold's home, to keep from being overheard. Even there, a detective walked up one day and demanded Royce's identification.

Royce said Arnold had cancelled his Thailand vacation before posting bail. Arnold's pair of one-way tickets to Thailand had a departure date of October 15th, for what Arnold said was going to be a 28-day vacation. Arnold said he went to Thailand every year at this time. But Royce said Arnold had never been to the country.

Upon leaving the jailhouse on Wednesday, Arnold declared, "They can say what they want, I am not a suspect. I had nothing to do with this Tylenol thing at all. This is more circumstance than anything."

Regarding his possession of cyanide, Arnold explained, "It just happens that they blew it out of proportion. I'm not saying what the chemicals were used for, but it was nothing illegal."

"I was willing to take a polygraph," Arnold added, "but my lawyer advised against it."

Arnold then said something that didn't seem to make sense at the time. "I knew the family, unfortunately, but not the suspect," he said. The identity of that suspect would become evident twelve days later.

Tyrone Fahner described Arnold's arrest as "another one of those [incidents] that are unrelated" to the killings. However, nine days after Arnold was released from jail, it became clear that Fahner did in fact view Arnold as a suspect.

21

A Conspiracy Theory

On Friday, October 22, 1982, Tyrone Fahner set up weekend negotiations with Thomas Royce to work out a deal with Roger Arnold in exchange for information he might have about the Tylenol murders. Three days later, the earlier portrayal of the Tylenol killer as a random murderer who did not know any of his victims suddenly changed.

Howard Fearon, Sr., the father of murder victim Lynn Reiner, was interrogated by the FBI and the Illinois Department of Law Enforcement (IDLE) on Sunday night, October 24th. The next morning, the early edition of the *Chicago Sun-Times* reported that investigators believed two men had conspired to commit the Tylenol murders. Authorities had questioned a prime suspect on Sunday night who was a relative of one of the victims. The victim and the victim's relative reportedly had a violent argument in late September before the poisonings occurred. Investigators said they believed this relative—possibly acting with another person—had placed cyanide-tainted Extra Strength Tylenol capsules on the shelves of Chicago area stores to give the appearance that the targeted relative was one victim of several random murders. The *Sun-Times* further reported that the prime suspect was a "long-time friend" of Roger Arnold.

On Monday evening, NBC's *Nightly News* specifically named Roger Arnold as one of the alleged co-conspirator in the Tylenol murders case. Two weeks earlier, police had said that one of the coincidences that made Arnold a suspect was that he worked with a relative of one of the victims. Now, with the disclosure of a Tylenol murder conspiracy theory, the relevance of that alleged relationship was more apparent. The local NBC affiliate in Chicago reported that Arnold and the victim's relative were "drinking buddies."

Investigators had evidently been trying to connect Roger Arnold to Howard Fearon, Sr., a truck driver for Jewel, ever since Arnold's arrest two weeks earlier. That was when the press had begun to cleverly place Fearon into their news stories, stating that Arnold worked with Fearon, a relative of one of the victims, i.e., one of the interesting coincidences that made Arnold a suspect. Fearon had been under around-the-clock surveillance since the beginning of the investigation.

Investigators from the FBI and IDLE had been trying to build a case against a relative of Lynn Reiner all along. They had hypothesized that one of Lynn's relatives had put the cyanide-laced Extra Strength Tylenol capsules into her bottle of Regular Strength Tylenol. This investigative strategy was alluded to by Roger Arnold, twelve days before the Tylenol murder conspiracy story broke, when he said, "I knew the family, unfortunately, but not the suspect."

The family Arnold mentioned was the Reiner family. And the only way Arnold could have known the identity of the suspect was if his interrogators had told him the suspect's name.

On Monday, October 25th, NBC reported that Roger Arnold's lawyer, Thomas Royce, had conducted weekend negotiations with Illinois Attorney General Tyrone Fahner. NBC quoted an unidentified high-ranking investigator as saying Royce was "trying to make a deal for Arnold" regarding information Arnold might have about the Tylenol case.

Royce said he only met with Fahner to try to find out why investigators were interested in Arnold. "He is the most innocent person you can imagine," Royce insisted.

It appeared that authorities were close to bringing indictments in the Tylenol murders case when Tom Brokaw opened NBC's Monday evening news broadcast by saying, "Chicago authorities now believe they know the real story behind the Tylenol murders. They're working on a substantial lead, but they're not yet prepared to make an arrest. However, the investigation, which has involved false leads and sensational developments which turn out not to be true does now appear to be going in one direction."

Jim Cummins, reporting for NBC in Chicago, said, "Investigators now believe the seven Tylenol murders were the work of two men, including the relative of one of the victims. Investigators believe the two men conspired to kill a member of the relative's family and cover up that crime by planting poisoned Tylenol in stores, killing other people to make it look like the work of a madman."

NBC did not identify the name of the victim's relative who was the suspect, but a law enforcement source in Washington said "members of the family of Mrs. Reiner were interviewed Monday," and "they have been very cooperative."

NBC showed video footage of an unidentified detective sitting in an unmarked car outside the home of the prime suspect. Tom Brokaw said this suspect—a relative of one of the victims—was under constant surveillance. However, the unmarked police car in the NBC video was not parked outside the home of Howard Fearon, Sr., as might have been expected based on prior news reports. It was instead parked outside the home of Lynn Reiner's husband, Ed Reiner. Fearon was a suspect; he just wasn't the prime suspect. Ed Reiner had been under around-the-clock surveillance since the beginning of the investigation. He had been the prime suspect all along.

Ed wasn't home when NBC shot that video footage outside his house late Monday afternoon. He had snuck out the back door to attend a meeting with agents from the FBI and IDLE. The press never specifically named Ed Reiner as a suspect, but they did set up camp outside his home, hoping to get the money-shot of police hauling him away in handcuffs.

IDLE investigators asked Ed to meet with them Monday, October 25th to help them out with the investigation. Agents from IDLE had already leaked the Tylenol murder conspiracy story on Sunday night so it would be headline news by the time they met with Reiner on Monday afternoon. The interrogation of Reiner, conducted by agents from the FBI and IDLE, went on for several hours, but it had barely begun when the interrogator's true objective hit Reiner like a sharp slap to the face. They wanted Reiner to confess to the Tylenol murders.

An IDLE investigator began the interrogation by declaring that Reiner had murdered his wife with cyanide-laced Extra Strength

Tylenol capsules. He also said that Reiner, with help from Roger Arnold, had planted bottles of cyanide-laced Tylenol capsules in Chicago-area supermarkets and drugstores. He said investigators knew that Reiner and Arnold were drinking buddies and that they had planned the Tylenol murder conspiracy at a bar on Chicago's North Side. The interrogator then falsely claimed that authorities even had photographs of Reiner and Arnold hanging out together at that bar.

Reiner was flabbergasted. He had never met Roger Arnold. He did not hang out in any bars on Chicago's North Side, and there were certainly no pictures of him and Arnold together at a North Side bar or anywhere else for that matter.

The IDLE agent spent an hour or more questioning Reiner before turning the interrogation over to the FBI. The FBI interrogator then made an astonishing revelation. The Tylenol murder conspiracy was not just a two-man conspiracy theory, as reported in the news media – it was a three-man conspiracy theory. The alleged co-conspirators were Ed Reiner, Roger Arnold, and Howard Fearon, Sr.

In a condescending, perverse tone, the FBI interrogator told Reiner that investigators knew that he, his father-in-law, and Roger Arnold were drinking buddies. The three of them, said the interrogator, killed Reiner's wife and then planted bottles of cyanide-laced Tylenol in local stores to make it look like Lynn's death was one of several random murders committed by a madman. The interrogator claimed that Reiner, Fearon, and Arnold were about to skip the country for Thailand when Arnold was picked up on October 11th. The interrogators did not tell Reiner that Arnold only had two tickets to Thailand.

As the inquisition dragged on, a sense of foreboding grew in Reiner's mind. He was rightfully apprehensive that his name was going to be plastered all over the media as the prime suspect. Several hours into the interrogation, the time was right to give Reiner a way out of his predicament. The interrogators offered Reiner the same deal they had given his father-in-law the previous day. One of the interrogators told Reiner that if he was innocent he could prove it by passing a lie detector test. To the consternation of his attorney,

Reiner agreed to take a polygraph exam, but he wanted the results made public right away.

Polygraph exams cannot produce evidence or solve crimes, but they are an applicable psychological weapon used by investigators to get confessions—sometimes false confessions. They were the primary "investigative tool" used by the members of the Tylenol task force who put many relatives of the Tylenol victims on the suspect list. The only way these relatives could get off that list was to take a polygraph exam. Law enforcement officials who had conducted an inept investigation were thus using polygraph exams because they had turned up no good leads. It was out of pure desperation that investigators from the FBI and IDLE interrogated Ed Reiner and accused him of being the ringleader of a Tylenol murder conspiracy.

After the grilling Reiner received from his interrogators, he probably was not in a very good state of mind to take a test designed to measure his level of anxiety. Nevertheless, Reiner knew that the allegations were ludicrous, and he wanted to put an end to them. Reiner had just passed the polygraph exam when the press began reporting about the discovery of an eighth bottle of cyanide-laced Extra Strength Tylenol capsules.

22

The Eighth Bottle

Jim Cummins, reporting for NBC News in Chicago on Monday, October 25, 1982, said investigators had learned of two more bottles of cyanide-laced Tylenol. "Investigators say that since the negotiations [between Tyrone Fahner and Roger Arnold's attorney] began, they've learned that at least two more bottles of cyanide contaminated Tylenol were planted in the Chicago area and have not yet been recovered," said Cummins. "And they now believe the cyanide used in the murders was purchased in a store in Racine, Wisconsin."

The two bottles not yet recovered were the eighth and ninth bottles of cyanide-laced Tylenol. The ninth bottle, which was apparently Lynn Reiner's unit-dose package of Extra Strength Tylenol capsules, was never mentioned again. The eighth bottle, however, became a major news story.

The eighth bottle of cyanide-laced Tylenol, reportedly purchased at Frank's Finer Foods, was discovered by laboratory technicians at the McNeil Consumer Products facility in Fort Washington. McNeil officials turned the contaminated bottle over to FBI agents who took the bottle to the FBI's lab in Washington D.C. for an extensive forensic analysis to detect fingerprints.

On Monday night, a law enforcement source in Washington said the eighth bottle of cyanide-laced Tylenol had been purchased by a woman from Winfield Township and turned in to police "some time ago, perhaps weeks ago," but was "just processed today." He said the bottle was sent with "a notation that it might be contaminated," and subsequent tests had confirmed the presence of cyanide.

The source said the woman had given the bottle to the Wheaton police who then mailed it to a lab operated by the McNeil Consumer

Products Company. However, the Wheaton police actually mailed the bottle to the Maple Plain Company, which then mailed it to McNeil. The Maple Plain Company, based in Maple Plain, Minnesota, was handling the reverse distribution of Tylenol capsules.

Reverse distribution is industry terminology for the collection and return of merchandise to the manufacturer. When consumers mailed their Tylenol capsules to the Maple Plain Company, the company sent them a coupon for $2.50 toward the purchase of a replacement Tylenol product. The returned bottles of Tylenol were then shipped to McNeil headquarters in Fort Washington where, with the exception of the eighth bottle of cyanide-laced Tylenol, they were destroyed.

Previously, the Wheaton police, just like the other Chicago-area police departments, had been forwarding all bottles of Extra Strength Tylenol capsules turned in by local residents to Johnson & Johnson's distribution center in Lemont, Illinois. Indeed, the seventh bottle of cyanide-laced Tylenol was discovered by J&J toxicologists at the company's temporary lab in Lemont just four days before the eighth bottle of cyanide-laced Tylenol was discovered by J&J lab workers at the McNeil plant in Fort Washington, Pennsylvania.

In mailing the eighth bottle to the Maple Plain Company, the Wheaton police simply followed the directive in the "Dear Doctor" letter that J&J had sent to retailers and wholesalers on October 13th. The "Dear Doctor" letter, written by McNeil Medical Director Dr. Thomas Gates, said in part:

> In response to this rapidly changing situation, McNeil has established the following policy pertaining to hospital, wholesale, and retail customers and consumers:

> In agreement with the FDA, McNeil Consumer Products Company is voluntarily withdrawing all non-blistered TYLENOL® capsule products (including Regular Strength TYLENOL® Capsules, Extra-Strength TYLENOL Capsules, non-blistered CoTYLENOL® Capsules, and Maximum-Strength TYLENOL® Sinus Medication

Capsules) from hospital, wholesale, and retail accounts nationally…... Consumers are urged to return all TYLENOL capsule products to the place of purchase, or to mail bottles to Tylenol Exchange, P.O. Box 2000, Maple Plains, Minnesota 55348.

In a statement given Monday night to the City News Bureau of Chicago, Tyrone Fahner said the eighth bottle of cyanide-laced Tylenol was from Lot MC2873 and had been purchased at the Frank's Finer Foods in Wheaton. The next day, however, Wheaton Police Lieutenant Terry Mee insisted that the woman who turned in the eighth bottle said she had purchased it at the Frank's Finer Foods store in Winfield, not Wheaton.

Mee said the woman brought the bottle in to the police station on October 13th and identified herself as the wife of a DuPage County Circuit Court judge. The woman "definitely said she bought [the eighth bottle] in Winfield sometime in the past. We are speculating that she bought it one to two weeks earlier," said Mee. "She told us she intended to turn it in right after [the Tylenol murders story] broke, but that she just let it go by."

Since there seemed to be some confusion about where the eighth bottle was purchased, the sensible thing to do was to ask the woman who had turned the bottle in, Marylou Walter, where she bought it. But that posed another problem. When the FBI interviewed Marylou, she told them she was not the person who had turned in the eighth bottle.

"We don't know why [the woman who did turn the bottle in] used that name, and now we are obviously concerned with determining who that person is," said Lieutenant Mee. "We are looking for a woman between 40 and 50 years old."

On Wednesday afternoon, October 27th, the woman who actually *had* turned in the eighth bottle called the Wheaton Police Department and identified herself as Linda Morgan; the wife of Judge Lewis Morgan, Jr. Wheaton Police Chief Carl Dobbs said a "clerical error" had led to the incorrect identification of the "mystery woman" as the wife of Judge Duane Walter. Judge Walter and Judge Morgan were both judges in the 18th Circuit Court in DuPage County.

Linda Morgan said she had purchased the Tylenol on the morning of the murders, but that she didn't turn it in to the Wheaton police until October 14th. "I believe now in the theory that if God wants you to go, it's going to be your turn; and for some reason it wasn't mine," said Morgan. "We had discovered the news of the poisonings the next day [the day after the poisonings] and we put it [the Tylenol] aside." She said family matters prevented her from turning in the bottle earlier, but she never revealed what those family matters were.

Fahner held a news conference on Wednesday, October 27th and provided an update on the forensic analysis of the cyanide-laced capsules from the eighth bottle. Earlier that day, an unidentified source in Washington said the FBI had found a fingerprint on the inside flap of the box from the eighth bottle. Fahner now said the FBI had also found a fingerprint on a capsule inside the eighth bottle and that the results from those fingerprint tests were about to be released. Fahner then proclaimed, "[we are] closer than we have ever been" to solving the Tylenol murders case.

Later that day, Linda Morgan came forward and revealed that she had opened the box for the eighth bottle, as well as the bottle itself. Amazingly, Morgan said she had even opened one of the capsules inside the eighth bottle. "I opened the capsule," Morgan confessed. She said later that the Tylenol didn't look odd.

However, if the Tylenol capsules in the eighth bottle did not look odd, then why did the Wheaton police mail the bottle with a note stating the capsules might be contaminated? According to Tyrone Fahner, the cyanide-laced capsules in Morgan's Tylenol bottle *did* look odd.

"The [eighth] bottle is clearly different than the other seven," said Fahner. "Some [of the cyanide-laced Tylenol capsules] were put together unartfully." Fahner said the poisoned medicine in the capsules from the eighth bottle had an "orangish" color, whereas the contents in the cyanide-laced capsules from the other seven bottles were off-white in color. In addition, the poisoned capsules in the eighth bottle contained a mixture of cyanide and acetaminophen, but the poisoned capsules in all the other bottles were filled completely with cyanide, containing only trace levels of acetaminophen.

The condition of the cyanide-laced capsules in the eighth bottle provided additional evidence that these capsules were not the work of the Tylenol killer. The cyanide-laced Tylenol capsules in the Kellerman and Janus bottles, inspected one day after the murders, were "swollen and discolored," the result of corrosion caused by moist cyanide. The cyanide-laced capsules in the seventh bottle were in an "advanced state of deterioration" when inspected 22 days after the murders. Conversely, the cyanide-laced Tylenol capsules in the eighth bottle, inspected 26 days after the murders, showed no signs of corrosion at all.

Fahner said the cyanide-laced Tylenol capsules in the eighth bottle were "substantially different" from previous bottles. This difference suggested that this bottle "may be unrelated to the other bottles so far recovered," he said. The logical conclusion from these findings is that someone—not the Tylenol killer—put cyanide into seven of the Tylenol capsules in the eighth bottle sometime after the Tylenol murders.

The FBI said they never found a match for the fingerprint on the eighth bottle's box-top flap, and they were unable to get a usable fingerprint from any of the capsules inside the bottle. Fahner said the prints on those capsules were smudged.

23

The Conspiracy

Ever since investigators had found the poisoned Extra Strength Tylenol capsules in Lynn Reiner's Regular Strength Tylenol bottle, they had been working under the assumption that Ed Reiner had somehow gotten those cyanide-laced capsules into a Tylenol bottle at the Frank's Finer Foods store in Winfield. This strategy had become more apparent on October 8th when NBC reported that investigators believed that someone, in a deliberate effort, had gone to the Frank's Finer Foods store in Winfield specifically to plant a bottle of cyanide-laced Tylenol in that store.

This NBC report went on to imply that the Tylenol killer knew in advance that Lynn Reiner would go to Frank's Finer Foods on the afternoon of the murders where, "as usual," she would buy a bottle of Regular Strength Tylenol. However, it was not usual at all for Lynn to buy Regular Strength Tylenol, or any pain medication. The Reiners used pain medication only occasionally.

It made no sense that someone who intended to murder Lynn Reiner would plant eight red and white Extra Strength Tylenol capsules, only five containing cyanide, into a bottle of gray and white Regular Strength Tylenol capsules. This scenario would have required Lynn to purchase the one and only bottle of cyanide-laced Tylenol capsules that the killer had supposedly planted at Frank's Finer Foods for her to buy.

This implausible scenario relied completely on luck and would have been extremely difficult to sell to a jury. To remedy this problem, local authorities may have planted the evidence they needed—the eighth bottle of cyanide-laced Tylenol—to get the conviction they wanted. The Wheaton police claimed that the eighth bottle of cyanide-laced Tylenol was purchased at the Frank's Finer Foods store in Winfield on September 29th. But it wasn't.

What the local authorities did not know then—and what they still may not know today—is that it would have been impossible for anyone to purchase the eighth bottle of cyanide-laced Tylenol at any of the Frank's Finer Foods stores. All of the Tylenol shipped to the Frank's Finer Foods stores was manufactured at McNeil's plant in Round Rock, Texas. But the Tylenol in the eighth bottle of cyanide-laced Tylenol was manufactured at McNeil's plant in Fort Washington, Pennsylvania.

As described earlier, the lot numbers for the Tylenol manufactured in Fort Washington began with two alpha characters followed by four numeric characters. The lot numbers for the Tylenol manufactured in Round Rock began with four numeric characters followed by two alpha characters. The first numeric digit in the lot numbers for Tylenol manufactured in Round Rock was "1", whereas the first numeric digit in the lot numbers for Tylenol manufactured in Fort Washington was "2". The Tylenol in the eighth bottle of cyanide-laced Tylenol, bearing lot number MC2873, was thus manufactured in Fort Washington.

The Tylenol manufactured in McNeil's Fort Washington plant was distributed only through J&J's regional distribution center in Montgomeryville, Pennsylvania. Whereas the Tylenol manufactured in McNeil's Round Rock plant was distributed through J&J's regional distribution centers in Round Rock, Texas; Montgomeryville, Pennsylvania; and Glendale, California.

An investigation completed by Johnson & Johnson and the Winfield police on October 1, 1982 revealed that Frank's Finer Foods received its Tylenol from the Certified Grocers distribution center in Hodgkins, Illinois. Winfield Police Officer Scott Watkins testified at Lynn Reiner's coroner's inquest that the Dependable Trucking Company delivered Tylenol to the Certified Grocers distribution center in Hodgkins. The California-based Dependable Trucking Company had shipped that Tylenol from a warehouse in California that received its Tylenol from J&J's regional distribution center in Glendale, California. J&J's Glendale distribution center received its Tylenol from the McNeil manufacturing plant in Round Rock.

All of the Tylenol in the Frank's Finer Foods store in Winfield, including the bottle of Regular Strength Tylenol from Lot 1833MB that Lynn Reiner purchased there, had been manufactured in Round Rock. The Tylenol in the eighth bottle of cyanide-laced Tylenol, bearing lot number MC2873, had been manufactured in Fort Washington. Linda Morgan could not have purchased that bottle at Frank's Finer Foods, because there was never a bottle of Tylenol with lot number MC2873 sitting on the shelves of any of the Frank's Finer Foods stores.

The eighth bottle of cyanide-laced Tylenol may have been planted into evidence by someone who wanted to give prosecutors a story implicating Ed Reiner as the Tylenol killer. Investigators knew that Ed could not have put the cyanide-laced Extra Strength Tylenol capsules into Lynn's Regular Strength Tylenol bottle after she returned home from Franks Finer Foods, because Ed wasn't home at the time. When Ed arrived with his 8-year-old daughter Michelle, Lynn was already dying from the poisoned capsule she'd swallowed minutes earlier. If officials were going to charge Ed Reiner for the Tylenol murders, they needed to come up with a story of how he could have gotten the cyanide-laced Extra Strength Tylenol capsules into a bottle of Regular Strength Tylenol at Frank's Finer Foods.

Prosecutors might have claimed that the Tylenol killer knew in advance that Lynn was going to buy Tylenol at Frank's Finer Foods on Wednesday afternoon and had thus gone to that store earlier and planted a bottle of cyanide-laced Extra Strength Tylenol capsules, which, according to Lieutenant Terry Mee, was the eighth bottle of cyanide-laced Tylenol. Then, taking this conjecture further; when the killer learned on Wednesday afternoon that Lynn was going to buy a bottle of *Regular Strength* Tylenol, he rushed back to Frank's Finer Foods and put cyanide-laced Extra Strength capsules into a Regular Strength Tylenol bottle. This hypothesis stretches the boundaries of plausibility, but the FBI and IDLE had in fact accused Ed Reiner of being the ringleader of a premeditated Tylenol murder conspiracy involving his father-in-law and Roger Arnold. For this conspiracy theory to be even remotely believable, officials had to explain how

Ed could have gotten the poisoned Extra Strength Tylenol capsules into Lynn's bottle of Regular Strength Tylenol sometime before she purchased it at Frank's Finer Foods. And they had to also explain why the Tylenol killer would put cyanide-laced Extra Strength capsules into a bottle of Regular Strength Tylenol.

The *Chicago Sun-Times* reported on Tuesday, October 26th that a man previously considered the prime suspect (Reiner) in the Tylenol investigation had been cleared after passing a lie detector test. However, officials said he did remain under scrutiny, but not as the person who poisoned the Extra Strength Tylenol capsules. Officials said [Reiner] had been cooperating with investigators, and he might take another lie test. Though Reiner had already passed a lie detector test, the FBI and IDLE clearly had not dismissed him as a suspect just yet.

When Linda Morgan came forward on October 27th and said she had purchased the eighth bottle at the Frank's Finer Foods store in Wheaton, instead of Winfield, the gig was up. The eighth bottle of cyanide-laced Tylenol could no longer be linked to the Winfield store, so it could no longer be used to advance the Tylenol murder conspiracy case authorities were trying to build against Ed Reiner.

Authorities in DuPage County were apparently prepared to enter the eighth bottle of cyanide-laced Tylenol as evidence if prosecutors decided to bring murder charges against Reiner. DuPage County had two highly publicized and politicized murder cases in the early 1980s: The Tylenol murders case and the Jeanine Nicarico murder five months later. In both cases, fabricated evidence was presented by DuPage County officials as if it was actual evidence. In the Tylenol case the fabricated evidence was the eighth bottle of poisoned Tylenol; in the Nicarico case it was an alleged confession.

Prosecutors from the DuPage County State's Attorney's Office charged Rolando Cruz and Alex Hernandez in 1983 for the rape and murder of ten-year-old Jeanine Nicarico. DuPage County detectives working on the Nicarico case hid exculpatory evidence that should have exonerated Cruz and Hernandez. They made up a so-called vision statement, claiming it was Cruz's confession to the Nicarico murder. That phony confession was the centerpiece of a prosecution that led to the wrongful convictions and death sentences for Cruz and Hernandez in 1985. During a lengthy appeals process, the defense won a second and then a third re-trial for each of the defendants.

DuPage County prosecutors pursued the third trials against Cruz and Hernandez even though their own forensic expert had found that the DNA evidence on the victim's body matched the DNA of Brian Dugan, a man who had confessed to the murder and rape of Jeanine, and who had previously raped and murdered two other girls in DuPage County. Rolando Cruz's third trial was a bench trial before Judge Ronald Mehling in 1995. Judge Mehling put a stop to the trial before the defense even presented their case. Mehling found Cruz not guilty after hearing jail-house snitches for the prosecution recant their original testimony and after the testimony of a lieutenant for the DuPage County Sheriff's Department revealed that Cruz's alleged confession had been made up by two of his deputies. Hernandez was also absolved a few weeks later.

In the 1980s and 1990s, Illinois was a hotbed of wrongful prosecution in death penalty cases. In 2004, of the 289 men and women sentenced to death in Illinois since 1977, eighteen had been exonerated and released from prison – an error rate of over six percent. Fourteen others had won reversals and were awaiting retrials or re-sentencing. The Illinois Governor's Commission on Capital Punishment found that these wrongful convictions were not the result of innocent mistakes, but rather the product of the deliberate actions of prosecutors and law enforcement authorities in Illinois who knowingly engaged in falsifying evidence, extracting coerced confessions, and relying on the testimony of jailhouse snitches. These tactics were used by government officials who were under pressure to solve big cases in order to advance their careers and achieve their political goals.

Tyrone Fahner, especially, felt the pressure to close out the Tylenol murders investigation quickly. His mentor, Governor Jim Thompson, was in a close gubernatorial race against Democrat challenger Adlai Stevenson, III. Fahner, in his race for Illinois attorney general, was trailing the Democrat challenger, Neil Hartigan. However, Fahner's standing in the polls had improved greatly since he'd become the official spokesperson of the Tylenol task force and was seen on television every day.

"[Fahner] probably had more than the necessary number of press conferences…to get him on the news each night," Chicago Police Superintendent Richard Brzeczek said later. "Fahner was running for election and nobody knew who he was, and they all figured, 'we'll get this solved and Ty will get a feather in his cap.'"

The Tylenol murder conspiracy scenario looked like a desperate effort to solve the case, make some arrests, and give Fahner the feather in his cap he needed to win the election. For the first 26 days of the Tylenol murders investigation, authorities had pursued an investigative strategy based on the erroneous hypothesis that six of the murders were staged as part of a conspiracy to cover up one premeditated murder. The evidence that likely would have revealed the true extent of the tamperings—the Tylenol capsules from Chicago area-stores—was destroyed. In addition, every bottle of cyanide-laced Tylenol recovered after the Tylenol murders, was engulfed by incredulous stories, unsubstantiated claims, and improbable circumstances.

Officials from the Tylenol task force said that Johnson & Johnson, while inspecting Tylenol capsules in October 1982, had discovered two bottles of cyanide-laced Tylenol—the seventh and eighth bottles. The eighth bottle was planted into evidence two weeks after the Tylenol murders, and the seventh bottle wasn't discovered until sixteen days after it had been turned over to Johnson & Johnson. Furthermore, authorities claimed to have initially misidentified the person who supposedly turned in the eighth bottle, and they never identified the person who turned in the seventh bottle.

The sixth bottle of cyanide-laced Tylenol—the first one not from one of the Tylenol victims—was discovered among the Tylenol bottles removed from the Osco Drug store in Woodfield Mall. Officials initially said they had found two bottles of cyanide-laced Tylenol at the Osco store, but then changed that story, claiming to have found only one contaminated bottle. *The Daily Herald* and the *New York Times* both reported that two unsold bottles of poisoned Tylenol were removed from the Osco Drug store in

Woodfield Mall. FDA Deputy Director Mark Novitch later confirmed that two bottles of cyanide-laced Tylenol had in fact been recovered from Osco Drug.

The news stories generated by the discovery of the eighth bottle of cyanide-laced Tylenol helped to bury the true source of Lynn Reiner's unit-dose package of cyanide-laced Extra Strength Tylenol capsules—the hospital. With the source of the cyanide-laced Tylenol that killed Lynn Reiner obscured, an important piece of evidence linking the tamperings to a warehouse in the Tylenol distribution network was also kept hidden.

Even if the authorities wanted to go back and track the cyanide-laced Tylenol capsules to a central point in the distribution channel—it was too late. Investigators had turned over the most important evidence they had—the Tylenol capsules themselves—to Johnson & Johnson, the one entity with both the incentive and the resources to eliminate evidence linking the tamperings to a location within the company's distribution network.

Tyrone Fahner was compelled to call a news conference on October 27th to put the final nail in the coffin of the Tylenol murder conspiracy story. He told reporters that Ed Reiner had voluntarily taken, and passed, a lie detector test. "No Reiner family member is a suspect in the Tylenol murders or any other investigation," said Fahner. The Tylenol murder conspiracy, which had been such a sensational story on Monday, October 25th, was now dead in the water two days later.

24

The Last Suspect

Authorities, by clearing Ed Reiner and Howard Fearon, Sr., and dropping the investigation of Roger Arnold, had cut Fahner's list of suspects to one name—Kevin Masterson. Though Masterson had not previously been named as a suspect, he was thrust into the limelight on November 1, 1982—one day before the Illinois election for attorney general and governor.

One investigator who insisted on anonymity said Masterson had told friends in September 1982 that he had planned to settle a grudge against two stores where the poisoned Tylenol was bought. Investigators told the *Chicago Tribune* that these friends had quoted Masterson as saying, "Now is the time to even the score" against Jewel Food and Frank's Finer Foods. The reference to Frank's Finer Foods was not a direct quote, and appears to have been yet another effort by un-named sources to erroneously link cyanide-laced Tylenol to Frank's Finer Foods. The manager of Frank's Finer Foods in Wheaton, one of four stores in the independently owned chain, said he had "no idea" how such a grudge might have originated.

An affidavit filed in the 18th Circuit Court in DuPage County said Masterson's anger toward Jewel arose from an incident in which his former wife, Joann, felt Jewel security officers had mistreated her after holding her for suspected shoplifting. Jane Armstrong, a vice president at Jewel, confirmed that the woman filed a civil suit against Jewel in 1975 and that a settlement was reached four years later. Armstrong refused to give details about the suit, but the *Chicago Tribune* said Mrs. Masterson had settled for $8,000.

In December 1982, Masterson's parents spoke to *The Daily Herald* about the havoc caused by the intense media focus. "I feel

[Kevin] was used, definitely by the media and others," said Kevin's father, John Masterson. The country's Founding Fathers designed a system of "trial by jury and you are innocent until proven guilty," Masterson stated. "The way things are today, it's trial by media, and you are guilty until proven innocent."

"The injustice done was so gross," said Kevin's mother, "that I think some strong positive statement should be made. You can't imagine the harm. Possibly the media could be made aware of the suffering this could cause a family. An individual is really at the mercy of the press."

The Mastersons said their son was never a suspect in the murders, and it "was more than coincidental" that daily press conferences were held by Tyrone Fahner during the week before the November 2nd election.

Even the feds refused to call Kevin Masterson a suspect. A Washington-based law enforcement source who asked not to be identified told the *Chicago Tribune*, "There's still nothing to indicate Masterson is anything other than a guy with a big mouth. There are some questions to ask him, but it would take a quantum leap from what is known to connect him to the Tylenol killings."

A well-timed news story hinting that Governor Thompson's attorney general was closing in on the Tylenol killer could only have helped the election outcomes for both Fahner and Thompson. The story leaked to the press on November 1st, implicating Masterson as a suspect, was well-timed, but did not give Fahner the popularity boost he needed.

On November 2nd, Tyrone Fahner lost his election bid. James Thompson narrowly defeated Adlai Stevenson. Kevin Masterson, in California at the time, soon turned himself in and was eliminated as a suspect.

Fahner had said on October 9th that his list of suspects had been reduced to just three people. Those people were Ed Reiner, Howard Fearon, Sr., and Kevin Masterson. Roger Arnold wasn't added to that list until one or two days later.

Long after the Tylenol murders case had gone cold, the rhetoric from Fahner, IDLE Commander Thomas Schumpp, Assistant U.S. Attorney Jeremy Margolis, and U.S. Attorney Dan Webb indicated that James Lewis was one of those announced prime suspects. But that wasn't the case. Authorities didn't identify Lewis as the writer of the extortion letter until October 13, 1982.

Roger Arnold, arguably the only legitimate suspect in the Tylenol murders case, appeared in court for a hearing on the unregistered gun charges near the end of October, but the judge postponed the hearing until a month later. Thomas Royce said the postponement was a delay tactic to keep Arnold under surveillance. Royce said he and his client were being harassed, and Arnold should be charged with the murders, or the police should back off. The police did back off, ending their surveillance and investigation of Arnold on October 27th.

When Arnold was questioned in mid-October about the Tylenol murders, he had threatened to take vengeance against the man who gave police the tip that led to his arrest. Chicago Police Sergeant Monroe Vollick said Arnold told him that "he sure would like to be in on the homicide of that man, the person that had informed on him, and to put him through what he was going through." Even so, Vollick said of Arnold, "I consider him a goof. One of those macho types who is into guns and making poisons, but not the Tylenol murders." Vollick would soon learn that Arnold did indeed have what it took to be a cold-blooded killer.

Chicago police said that on June 18, 1983, Arnold, after a night of drinking, sought revenge against Marty Sinclair, the man who had turned him in. Arnold was outside a Lincoln Avenue bar on Chicago's North Side when the man who was the focus of his anger emerged from that bar a couple hours after midnight. Arnold approached the man and the two spoke briefly before Arnold shot him in the chest. The bullet went straight through the man's heart, allowing him only seconds to cry out, "I'm shot," before he died. One of the witnesses chased Arnold to a getaway car and was able to get the license plate number before the car sped off.

As it turned out, Arnold had not murdered Marty Sinclair. He had actually killed John Stanisha, a 46-year-old computer consultant and father of three.

A Cook County grand jury indicted Arnold for murder and armed violence. Prosecutors for the Cook County state's attorney's office said that Arnold had mistaken John Stanisha for Marty Sinclair. They called the shooting a revenge murder, but Arnold and his attorney, Thomas Royce, said otherwise.

Royce denied that Arnold mistook Stanisha for the person who told police that Arnold had cyanide in his apartment. "That couldn't be further from the truth," insisted Royce, who said he was with Arnold the entire time he was being questioned about murdering Stanisha. Arnold "made no statements to anybody," said Royce. "We don't know who the informant was in the Tylenol case."

In fact, Arnold must have known that Marty Sinclair was the informant. After Arnold's arrest on October 11, 1982, Chicago Police Detective Jerry Beam told reporters that the bartender who told police that Arnold kept cyanide at his home was the same man who had recently charged Arnold with assault. Arnold knew that Sinclair had charged him with aggravated assault, so he must have also known that Sinclair provided police with the tip that made him a suspect in the Tylenol murders case.

It's also untrue that Arnold mistook Stanisha for Sinclair. Roger Arnold and Marty Sinclair knew each other fairly well. Arnold was a frequent patron at Sinclair's tavern. Four months prior to the Tylenol murders, Sinclair filed assault charges against Arnold after Arnold had pulled a gun on him. They engaged in a conversation at Sinclair's bar in early October just before Sinclair dropped a dime on Arnold.

Arnold testified that Stanisha had taunted him in the bar about being arrested in the Tylenol murders case. Arnold later returned to the bar with revenge on his mind. Arnold said he intended to frighten Stanisha, but not kill him. He said that a bullet had accidentally discharged from the gun. The jury didn't believe Arnold's story; they convicted him in 1984 for the murder of John Stanisha. Arnold was sentenced to 30 years in prison.

When Roger Arnold murdered John Stanisha, he revealed himself as a killer. But was he the Tylenol killer?

In a nine-page synopsis of the Tylenol murders probe, IDLE Investigator Richard Tetyk wrote that Roger Arnold told his supervisor at Jewel that he was "mad at people and wanted to throw acid at them or poison them." A few days before the Tylenol murders, Arnold purchased two one-way tickets to Thailand with a departure date of October 15, 1982. A little more than a week after the Tylenol murders, Arnold, while holding a bag of white powder that he said was cyanide, walked into several North Side taverns and talked about killing people with cyanide. Arnold kept cyanide in the basement of his house until just prior to the Tylenol murders.

A substantial amount of circumstantial evidence makes Arnold a valid suspect in the Tylenol murders case, but no one ever suggested a possible motive. "One of the most sensational murder cases in this century has gone unsolved because the person who did it randomly killed seven people," remarked former U.S. Attorney Dan Webb. "If you have no motive, if all you're doing is killing people for no reason whatsoever, then that is likely to be the most perfect murder because there won't be any ties back to you."

There are, however, a couple of obvious motives that can be ascribed to Roger Arnold. For starters, he was angry at people in general and was prone to violence. Arnold had talked about poisoning people and allegedly had threatened to kill his estranged wife with cyanide capsules.

Thomas Royce referred to Arnold as "a soldier of fortune type guy." Arnold apparently adhered to the ideology of *posse comitatus*, a loosely organized far-right social movement that opposes the United States federal government, believes in radical localism, and engages in paramilitary training. Arnold's literature included *The Anarchist Cookbook*, an instruction manual for making explosives; a stash of *Soldier of Fortune* magazines; and a copy of *The Poor Man's James Bond*, a survivalist manual containing instructions for using cyanide-filled capsules to make lethal weapons. The vast majority of people who own these magazines and books are, of course, law-abiding citizens. However, it is also true that these publications were standard fare among adherents of the *posse comitatus* movement in 1982 whose leaders had stockpiled cyanide and advocated mass murder in a war against Jews and "Jew sympathizers."

If prosecutors had brought a case against Arnold, they likely would have characterized his statements about poisoning people with cyanide as a confession to the Tylenol murders. Charging Arnold with the murders might have allowed authorities to close out the case as the work of an angry man who had put cyanide-laced capsules into Tylenol bottles at the retail stores—unless an investigation of Arnold would have debunked this approved theory and unearthed evidence of Johnson & Johnson's liability for the tamperings.

Bob Fletcher, a spokesman for the Illinois Department of Law Enforcement, commented in 1986 on the failure of investigators to capture the Tylenol killer. "Of course, the killer could have been operating on a completely rational plan that we simply don't perceive yet," remarked Fletcher. "It's enormously frustrating."

Fletcher's frustration may have been the byproduct of an investigation that assumed that the Tylenol killer had planted the cyanide-laced Tylenol capsules in Chicago-area retail stores, ignoring the evidence pointing to a warehouse within the Tylenol distribution network as the source of those poisoned capsules.

25

Project Chatham

Johnson & Johnson's handling of the Tylenol crisis quickly became the primary case study that experts in the public relations industry now point to as the perfect example of how a widely publicized crisis should be handled. "The Tylenol crisis is without a doubt the most exemplary case ever known in the history of crisis communications," proclaimed public relations expert Ten Berge. "Any business executive who has ever stumbled into a public relations ambush ought to appreciate the way Johnson & Johnson responded to the Tylenol poisonings. They have effectively demonstrated how major business has to handle a disaster."

One financial analyst on Wall Street said, "Johnson & Johnson management was quick to cast themselves in the role of the self-sacrificing servants of the people. They generated enormous public sympathy and managed to convince most Tylenol consumers that they (the people) owed the company cooperation in saving the product."

"Within one year, thanks to the intrinsic fairness of the public, Tylenol was back to its former pre-eminent position in the market," said Larry Foster, J&J's vice president of public relations. "That seemingly impossible marketing achievement became a reality because the public realized that the company was not to blame for the tragedy, and because the press felt that the crisis had been handled with skill and in the public interest."

"No disasters of this magnitude are handled flawlessly," Foster said, "but by public and professional acclaim, Tylenol is still viewed as the classic example of how to manage a crisis. And the abiding interest in these heinous crimes, even today, is nurtured by the fact that they remain unsolved."

"Perhaps because of the magnitude and complexity of the experience, those most closely involved in the Tylenol tragedy do not subscribe to the philosophy that a crisis plan on file assures successful management of a disaster," remarked Foster. "There was no such plan on file at J&J capable of guiding us through the months that followed the fateful morning of September 30, 1982 when we first learned of the Chicago murders."

J&J President David Clare said, "The events surrounding the Tylenol crisis were so atypical that we found ourselves improvising every step of the way."

In truth, the organizational changes Johnson & Johnson made in September of 1982 put the company in the ideal position to manage this particular crisis. It was indeed fortunate for Johnson & Johnson that just days before seven people died from cyanide-laced Tylenol capsules near David Collins's hometown of Oak Park, Illinois, James Burke had put Collins in charge of the company that manufactured and sold Tylenol.

Also in September 1982, J&J began to implement the recommendations of the company's "Project Chatham" Committee to centralize the contracting, order fulfillment, and distribution of J&J products, including Tylenol. Johnson & Johnson had initiated Project Chatham in 1981 to explore the idea of centralizing the sales and logistics functions of 13 major J&J operating companies. The Committee recommended in April 1981 that J&J should create an operating unit to consolidate the sales and logistics functions and provide a common customer service group and electronic order entry system.

Project Chatham sat dormant for the next 17 months. Then, in September of 1982, J&J formed the Hospital Services Group (HSG) as a transitional corporate unit to develop action plans to implement the recommendations of the Project Chatham Committee. HSG also took control of the distribution of raw materials and finished goods. Johnson & Johnson had thus begun to take control of the distribution channel in the same month that the cyanide-laced Extra Strength Tylenol capsules entered the distribution channel in Chicago.

The promotion of David Collins and the decision to centralize J&J's distribution and logistics functions occurred during, or just after, the company's annual planning review meeting when James Burke openly worried about the potential for a problem with the Tylenol business. "I took some kidding at that meeting for worrying about things I don't have to," recalled Burke. "We had been marveling at how lucky we were to be in our industry, to have some very profitable brands doing so well, and I had said, offhand, what if something happens to one of them, like Tylenol? Nothing is impregnable, but it was such an extraordinary business, there didn't seem to be any downside. Nobody could come up with anything."

When the cyanide poisoning deaths were linked to Tylenol, Johnson & Johnson took charge of the situation, and the FDA simply fell in line. FDA Deputy Director Mark Novitch described the FDA's response to the Tylenol murders as though the agency was merely a bystander, acting at the direction of James Burke. Novitch said:

> The actions that followed [the Tylenol murders] have become a case study in responsible crisis management. Major players were: Jim Burke, chairman of J&J; Dave Collins, chairman of McNeil, the J&J subsidiary responsible for Tylenol; Joe Chiesa, McNeil president; Tom Gates, its medical director; and many other colleagues. If they felt despair and uncertainty, none was apparent. Four decades earlier, J&J had adopted a credo stating the principles on which they would conduct their business. Burke and Collins said the credo told them what to do in the Tylenol crisis and it is impossible to say otherwise.
>
> J&J involved the FDA immediately and continuously. It withdrew the initial lots from which the tampered drugs came and then, in the wake of copycat tamperings, withdrew all Tylenol capsules even though both J&J and the FDA had determined that the tamperings did not occur in its plants. J&J kept the press and public fully informed and even put its chairman in the unaccustomed

role of chief company spokesperson. This was one of the first times that the CEO of a major company was used as a spokesperson for a crisis. This effort set a precedent that exists to this day.

Eight days after Burke learned about the Tylenol poisonings, he acknowledged that the original damage control group at corporate headquarters had evolved into three task forces that were working on an "image rescue project." One task force that concentrated on employee morale had already produced an hour-long videotape made up of news reports and comments by company officials. Burke, in this taped message, told his employees, "People don't blame us. They feel we are being victimized just like everyone else." J&J showed the tape on October 7, 1982 on the employee TV network.

Burke made up his mind on October 10th that all of Johnson & Johnson's 150 operating companies would pitch in and help re-launch the Tylenol brand. There would be no new name for the brand as some experts had recommended. "It will take time, it will take money, and it will be very difficult, but we consider it a moral imperative, as well as good business, to restore Tylenol to its preeminent position," proclaimed Burke.

Wayne Nelson, the co-founder of the McNeil Consumer Products Company, agreed. "It would almost be an admission of some kind of guilt in my opinion to walk away from [the Tylenol] name. We'd be very foolish. And even if a third of this business never came back, we'd still have the top-selling pain reliever in the world," said Nelson, "It's better than a sharp stick in the eye."

On Friday, October 22, 1982, the FDA sent a letter to Johnson & Johnson, officially clearing the company of any responsibility for the Tylenol tamperings. The letter, signed by Joseph Hile, the associate commissioner for regulatory affairs at the FDA, said:

> We conclude that the contamination did not occur at either [McNeil manufacturing] plant, and was the result of tampering after the capsules had been shipped to distribution points, and most likely after they reached the retail shelves.

Notably, the FDA did not rule out the distribution channel as the true source of the cyanide-laced Tylenol capsules. The FDA also never presented any information to support the tampering-in-the-retail-stores hypothesis.

Prior to re-launching Tylenol in tamper-resistant packaging, Burke hosted a pep rally for 2,259 sales representatives. He exhorted them to call on physicians and pharmacists and win back Tylenol's market share. By year's end, J&J sales representatives had made more than a million such presentations to promote the reintroduction of Tylenol. J&J gave out coupons for $2.50 off the purchase of any Tylenol product. McNeil sales reps recovered former stock levels of Tylenol capsules by implementing an off-invoice pricing program that provided retail companies with discounts linked to wholesale purchasing patterns established prior to October 1982. These discounts, known as performance-based rebates, went as high as 25 percent. J&J began running commercials on October 24, 1982 to promote the upcoming launch of Tylenol in tamper-resistant packaging.

"We ran a series of campaigns that said 'trust us,'" recalled Larry Foster. "We don't know what the answer is to this tragedy, but trust us. As soon as we find out what it is, we will tell you."

McNeil Medical Director Dr. Thomas Gates appeared in commercials, telling the public, "We want you to continue to trust Tylenol."

In mid-November 1982, the FDA ran a "public-service" ad in newspapers across the country to ease consumer fears about adulterated OTC drugs. Printed in bold type at the top of the ad was a heading that read: "A Public Service announcement about over-the-counter medicine." The subtitle read, "From Dr. Arthur H. Hayes, Commissioner, U.S. Food and Drug Administration."

The entire body of the ad was a personal commentary from Arthur Hayes, covering Johnson & Johnson's talking points, namely, that the tamperings could not have been anticipated and were done by a madman at the retail stores. Hayes said the poisonings were "a criminal tampering of medicine on store shelves... We've all been shocked by the incident." Hayes called Tylenol an "innocent product," and stated, "We can't guarantee protection against everything that a sick mind might think of."

Hayes closed his pitch by saying, "We don't have to do without the medicines that make our lives more comfortable."

Larry Foster predicted that consumers would realize "we were victimized along with society" and that because of goodwill generated by the 95-year-old Johnson & Johnson, "we may come out of this with a stronger image."

Johnson & Johnson emerged from the Tylenol crisis widely hailed as having provided a shining example of how to handle a major business calamity. Consumers remained loyal to Johnson & Johnson, and Tylenol retained its status as the country's top-selling OTC pain-reliever. *The New York Times* reported on December 24, 1982 that Tylenol had regained 24 percent of the market for pain relievers, not too far off the 37 percent share the product held before the crisis. Less than a year later, sales returned to their pre-crisis level.

26

Legacy

TIME magazine, in its decade-ending review of American business during the eighties, called Johnson & Johnson's handling of the Tylenol crisis, the "most applauded corporate response to a disaster." The company's "frank, decisive responses," according to *TIME*, "won back customer loyalty, and is now a textbook case in public relations."

Johnson & Johnson is portrayed still today as having been completely open and forthright with the press and the public on matters related to the Tylenol tamperings. An article that ran in *FORTUNE* magazine on May 22, 2007 said "Johnson & Johnson's response to the 1982 Tylenol poisonings remains the gold standard in crisis control."

Jack O'Dwyer, of O'Dwyer PR in New York City, is one of the few public relations experts to criticize this "gold standard" attributed to Johnson & Johnson for its handling of the Tylenol tamperings. An amicus brief filed in November 2002 on behalf of five public relations groups in Nike et al. v. Marc Kasky led O'Dwyer to call for some accuracy in the way the Tylenol murders case is taught in universities and portrayed in the media. The amicus brief has a fatal flaw, remarked O'Dwyer. It cited Johnson & Johnson's handling of the Tylenol murders as an example of ideal communication. The brief said, "Johnson & Johnson maintained an open dialogue with the press and public throughout the crisis."

In reality, Johnson & Johnson avoided the press, suppressed information regarding the lot numbers and distribution of the poisoned capsules, failed to disclose the existence of nearly 300 consumer complaints of Tylenol tamperings and contaminations in the three years prior to the cyanide poisonings, and waited six days before recalling all Tylenol capsules nationwide.

O'Dwyer said that Johnson & Johnson's public stance was that it had no special knowledge of the case and, therefore, had nothing to say to reporters in a press conference. O'Dwyer concludes: "J&J was just another case of normal corporate foot-dragging during a crisis."

"Although it took about a week for J&J to order the withdrawal [of Tylenol capsules], which was somewhat after the fact by that time," remarked O'Dwyer, "that is not how the withdrawal has entered public lore thanks to a massive advertising and PR campaign conducted by the company." Johnson & Johnson never held a press conference, but rather chose to handle some 1,500 press calls on an individual basis. "Probably nearly all of these were phone calls," said O'Dwyer. "Who knows what J&J told or didn't tell these individual reporters?"

J&J executives never publicly expressed sorrow for the Tylenol murders victims or their families, and they never uttered the names of any of the victims. Yet Larry Foster said that amid the hysteria Johnson & Johnson tried not to forget about the families of the victims. Ultimately though, he said he and his colleagues did not do as much for them as they could have. Foster said J&J originally considered the idea of setting up scholarships for the children affected by the deaths, but that proposal fell through.

The employees at McNeil's Fort Washington plant offered to provide $100 each toward a reward for whoever found the person who tampered with their product. McNeil employees wanted to help the victims' families with emotional support, counseling, and money from their own pockets. Foster said Johnson & Johnson executives rejected these generous offers because they were worried that any expression of compassion or offer of financial help might be construed as an admission of liability.

"We couldn't be as open with [the victims' families] as we wanted," remarked Foster, "because the lawyers held us back. They were trying to protect the company."

Product liability lawsuits filed on behalf of all seven Tylenol murders victims sought a total of $40.1 million from Johnson &

Johnson and the retailers that sold the poisoned Tylenol capsules. In July 1985, Judge Brian Duff, in the circuit court in Cook County, dismissed the retailers as defendants, but allowed the lawsuits against Johnson & Johnson to go forward, stating, "Even if the Tylenol manufacturers had no knowledge of cyanide in [their] product, they could still be held liable."

In January 1986, the lawsuits were transferred to a different circuit judge, the Honorable Brian Crowe, who granted the parties' motions for reconsideration on a number of issues. At a proceeding later that year, Judge Crowe granted the retailers' motion to make the dismissal orders final. The plaintiffs appealed this decision to the Illinois Supreme Court, which ruled in December 1987 that the state's product liability law allowed for the future reinstatement of the lawsuits against the retailers under certain circumstances, such as if the manufacturer could not be sued or an action against it would be unavailing.

Attorney Leonard Ring, who represented the estates of Adam and Stanley Janus, said the court's decision would allow lawyers to proceed with discovery motions in the lawsuits against Johnson & Johnson. "I foresee the cases going to trial by summer [1988]," he said. "Based on my conversations with Johnson & Johnson's attorneys, I think it is more likely we will go to trial rather than settle out of court." Both these predictions would be proven wrong.

The lawsuits remained in legal purgatory until September 14, 1990, when J&J's motion to dismiss the case due to lack of evidence was denied by Judge Donald O'Connell. The trial date was set for October 19, 1990 in the circuit court in Cook County. Johnson & Johnson immediately sought, and was granted, a continuance, delaying the start of the trial to Monday, May 13, 1991.

As the trial-date approached, J&J's lawyers filed a motion to secure a closed trial in the circuit court in Cook County, arguing before Judge Warren Wolfson that an open trial might spur copycat crimes. Judge Wolfson promptly denied J&J's motion for a secret trial.

Just two days before the start of the trial, J&J's lawyers, suddenly anxious to cut a deal, called the plaintiffs' attorneys late Saturday night, May 11, 1991, and offered to settle out of court.

Negotiations began immediately, with J&J's attorneys pressuring each of the plaintiffs to settle their individual Tylenol liability lawsuits, stating that if even one of them refused to sign a settlement agreement, the company would not settle any of their lawsuits.

The secret settlement negotiations continued through Monday morning, the day the trial was scheduled to begin, compelling Circuit Court Judge Warren Wolfson to announce that jury selection would be delayed until 1:30 p.m. One of the plaintiffs' attorneys, Phillip Corboy, said the delay had "to do with sorting out the exhibits—we have 150 of them, after all."

Settlement agreements with all the plaintiffs were finalized early Monday afternoon, May 13, 1991, thus keeping the lawsuits and the evidence from being presented in an open trial. Judge Wolfson then called the court to order shortly before 3:30 p.m. "The parties have resolved their differences," he announced. "The case has been settled. That ends the proceedings in this courtroom."

The plaintiffs and their lawyers were all required to sign confidentiality agreements to keep the terms of the settlements secret. "No one can talk about that," Corboy said. "Even the families don't know what the other families are getting."

According to the *Chicago Sun-Times*, some estimates put the settlement at close to $50 million. The actual amount was nowhere near that much. Based on settlement information provided by some of the Tylenol victims' relatives, the payments ranged from about $200,000 to $990,000 per victim. The average payment was in the neighborhood of $500,000 per victim, about $3.5 million in total. The plaintiffs' attorneys took 40 percent, leaving about $2.1 million to split up among the spouses, children, and parents of the seven victims.

Johnson & Johnson filed a motion for a protective order to seal all the documents that the company had turned over to the court. Judge Wolfson expressed distaste for this type of protective order, saying, "The public has a right to know about events that take place in courtrooms. Courts should not countenance (tolerate) the use of concealment as a bargaining chip." Wolfson then followed this judicious statement by granting J&J's motion for protection, ensuring that the public would never see any of the documents that Johnson & Johnson had turned over to the court.

With the product liability lawsuits resolved, J&J spokesperson Robert Kniffin trumpeted the company line. "Though there is no way we could have anticipated a criminal tampering with our product or prevented it," said Kniffin, "we wanted to do something for the families and finally get this tragic event behind us."

Plaintiffs' attorneys Corboy and Ring, smiling from their so-called megabuck victory, praised Johnson & Johnson for its quick action to change Tylenol's packaging once the deaths occurred. "They saw their duty and they did it. Now people can rest easy," declared Corboy. "Liability will never again be brought into the forefront," he said. "The public has already been protected. The product has been changed such that it will never happen again."

Regarding J&J's decision to settle the lawsuits; Corboy said, "It takes two to tango, and [Johnson & Johnson] filled out our dance card."

The Tylenol murders case, reduced years earlier to a case-study hyping the dubious legacy of Johnson & Johnson's gold standard of crisis management, had now been closed-out with the trite sound bites of happy attorneys who never really got justice for the victims or their families.

Epilogue

Near the end of 1982, Tyrone Fahner gave a rather pitiful assessment of the Tylenol murders investigation. "When all this is said and done," remarked Fahner, "the most interesting story to come out of this—outside of the terrible tragedy—will be that we drummed up every bit of scud walking around. We found the people who said they had done it, who had access to chemicals, who acted weird, who potentially were in the right place at the right time. And we did some incredibly fine investigative work... and we came up dry."

In January 1983, Thomas Schumpp, a commander for the Illinois Department of Law Enforcement, took over as the director and primary spokesperson for the skeletal remains of the Tylenol task force. By September 1983, the task force had dwindled to six FBI agents and six agents from the Illinois State Police. But they had no leads to investigate.

"With Tylenol there was never a message or a clue to the reason," said Schumpp. "Not only can't we say who, but we can't say why."

IDLE Commander Ed Cisowski even second guessed the decision to turn the Chicago-area Tylenol capsules over to Johnson & Johnson. "The crime scenes were hard to protect," said Cisowski. "Everything was taken off the shelves [in the product recall]. That made it hard. But that's about all she wrote."

Chicago Police Superintendent Richard Brzeczek said he doubted the case would ever be solved. "There's just nothing to tie anyone in to it," he explained. "You need some evidence."

"The thing is," said Brzeczek, "if someone walked in and said 'I am the cyanide killer, I did all of these things,' other than the admission on that person's part, there is no tangible evidence to tie

155

someone to it. It's all uncorroborated, and that doesn't hold up in court."

On the fifth anniversary of the Tylenol murders, a few Illinois authorities began telling reporters that James Lewis had been their prime suspect all along. "Lewis remains the best suspect we have," Schumpp declared.

In September 1992, Schumpp once again pegged Lewis as the Tylenol killer. "Over the years, my position has been that [Lewis] was the prime suspect, said Schumpp. "In my mind, he remains that. I personally believe he did it."

Yet Schumpp freely admitted that there was no evidence linking Lewis to the tamperings. "The problem is, said Schumpp, "if you don't have any physical evidence and it's only one or two people involved who keep their mouths shut, there's nothing you can do. Knowing something and proving it are sometimes a long way apart from one another."

For more than 26 years, government officials never indicated that they were following up on any real leads in the Tylenol murders case. Then, on February 4, 2009, the investigation was reactivated in a very public way when agents from the FBI and the Illinois State Police searched James Lewis's apartment while television news helicopters hovered overhead. The FBI said new tips and advances in forensic technology had spurred authorities to take a second look at all the evidence. This public reactivation of the Tylenol murders investigation was the product of an operation initiated many years earlier by a handful of Illinois and FBI officials who had pegged Lewis as the Tylenol killer. But did they have any real evidence?

The largely covert campaign by Illinois and FBI authorities to build a case against James Lewis for the Tylenol murders is the subject of the second book in the TYMURS series—*TYLENOL MAN: A 30-Year Quest to Close the Tylenol Murders Case*.

About the Author

Scott Bartz is the author of the TYMURS series:

TYMURS: The 1982 Tylenol Murders

TYLENOL MAN: A 30-Year Quest to Close the Tylenol Murders Case

TYMURS NYC: The 1986 Tylenol Murder (To be released October 20, 2012)

Bartz's first book, *The Tylenol Mafia: Marketing, Murder, and Johnson & Johnson*, was released in 2011.

Appendix: Statistical Analysis

The probability that one or more of the first seven capsules taken from McFarland's 50-count bottle would contain poison was 68 percent; calculated as follows:

43/50 x 43/49 x 43/48 x 43/47 x 43/46 x 43/45 x 43/44 = 86% x 86% x 85% x 85% x 85% x 85% x 84% = 32%; 100% - 32% = 68%

The following data is used to determine the probability that the very first dose taken from all four of the Kellerman, Reiner, Janus, and Prince Tylenol bottles would all contain cyanide:

Kellerman: 5 poisoned capsules in her 50-count bottle

Probability that the first dose (1 capsule) taken would contain cyanide = 10%:

(50 / 5) = 10%

Janus: 9 poisoned capsules in Janus's 50-count bottle (6 cyanide-laced capsules were found in Janus's bottle. Adam, Stanley, and Theresa Janus each swallowed 2 capsules. Medical examiners determined that each had swallowed one cyanide-laced capsule, so the bottle initially contained 9 cyanide-laced capsules).

Probability that the first dose (2 capsules) taken would contain cyanide = 36%

(9 / 50) + (9 / 49) = 36%

Reiner: 5 poisoned capsules in her 50-count bottle

Probability that the first dose (2 capsules) taken would contain cyanide = 19%

$$(5 \: / \: 50) + (5 \: / \: 49) = 19\%$$

Prince: 2 poisoned capsules in her 24-count bottle

Probability that the first dose (1 capsule) taken would contain cyanide = 8%

$$(2 \: / \: 24) = 8\%$$

The Probability that the first dose taken from all four of the Kellerman, Janus, Reiner, and Prince Tylenol bottles would contain a cyanide-laced capsule was 0.0547 percent, or 1 in 1,828, calculated as follows:

$$10\% \times 36\% \times 19\% \times 8\% = 0.0547\% = 1 \text{ in } 1,828$$

There was about an 18 percent probability, on average, that the first dose taken from the Kellerman, Janus, Reiner, and Prince bottles would contain cyanide. Using this average probability of 18 percent to calculate the odds that the first dose taken from all of those four bottles would all contain cyanide produces a slightly more conservative result of 0.105 percent:

$$18\% \times 18\% \times 18\% \times 18\% = 0.105\% = 1 \text{ in } 952$$

Endnotes

PART 1

1 A Premonition

1   It was shaping up: Moore, Thomas. "The Fight to Save Tylenol." *TIME*, November 29, 1982.

1   "I took some kidding": Moore, Thomas. "The Fight to Save Tylenol." *TIME*, November 29, 1982.

1   This foreshadowing event: Swanson, Al. Kane County Sherriff's Police General Report, October 1, 1982.

2   The words "EXTRA-STRENGTH": Associated Press. "Officials report some leads in cyanide case." *The Paris News*, October 4, 1982.

2   One of the boxes: Associated Press. "Officials report some leads in cyanide case." *The Paris News*, October 4, 1982.

2   In between: Dowling, John. "Cyanide Murders Hunt Has Dozen Suspects." *Ironwood Daily Globe*, Oct. 5, 1982 -- Malcolm, Andrew H. "Cyanide Case Focuses on Find in Parking Lot at All-night Restaurant." *New York Times*, October 5, 1982.

2   "It looked like": Dowling, John. "Cyanide Murders Hunt has Dozen Suspects." *Ironwood Daily Globe*, October 5, 1982.

2   Swanson examined a few: Cohen Sharon. "Tylenol found in lot were tampered with." Syracuse Herald-Journal, October 4, 1982. -- Malcolm, Andrew H. "Cyanide Case Focuses on Find in Parking Lot at All-night Restaurant." *New York Times*, October 5, 1982. -- Associated Press. "Officials report some leads in cyanide case." *The Paris News*, October 4, 1982.

2   Swanson and Chavez got: Malcolm, Andrew H. "Cyanide Case Focuses on Find in Parking Lot at All-night Restaurant." *New York Times*, October 5, 1982

2   Death without Warning

5   Sixteen hours after: Beck, Melinda; Hagar, Mary; LaBreque, Ron; Monroe, Sylvester; Prout, Linda. "The Tylenol Scare." *Newsweek*, October 11, 1982. – Greene, Bob. "An Open Letter to the Tylenol Killer." *The Post-Standard*, October 22, 1982.

5   At about 7 a.m.: Beck, Melinda; Hagar, Mary; LaBreque, Ron; Monroe, Sylvester; Prout, Linda. "The Tylenol Scare." *Newsweek*, October 11, 1982. – Greene, Bob. "An Open Letter to the Tylenol Killer." The Post-Standard, October 22, 1982. -- Nenni, Pete; Van Wye, Joann. "5 dead after taking Tylenol capsules filled with cyanide." *The Daily Herald*, October 1, 1982.

6   In nearby Arlington Heights: Associated Press. "Poison Tylenol Kills Five." The Capital, October 1, 1982. -- Burris, Anne. "A string of coincidences linked Tylenol poisonings." The Daily Herald, October 1, 1982. -- Associated Press. "Tylenol traces tale of tragedy." *Lawrence Journal-World*, October 3, 1982.

6   "Nothing seemed to help": Tifft, Susan; Lee, Griggs. "Poison Madness in the Midwest." *TIME*, October 11, 1982.

6   Around the same time: Daniel, Leon. "A Nightmare in capsule form." *Pacific Stars and Stripes*, October 12, 1982. -- *Nightly News*. NBC: October 8, 1982. -- Coroner's inquest, re: Lynn Reiner. Direct examination by DuPage County Coroner Richard Ballinger, 1982.

7   Michelle's most vivid memories. Rosen, Michelle. Telephone interview by author, 2010.

7   Shortly after Lynn was admitted: Turner, K L. Coroner's Report: Mary McFarland, September 30, 1982.

8   "I don't feel good guys": Turner, K L. Coroner's Report: Mary McFarland, September 30, 1982.

8   Mary McFarland and Lynn Reiner: Siekmann, Peter. DuPage County Coroner's Office Preliminary Report, re: Mary Reiner, September 30, 1982. -- Coroner's inquest, re: Lynn Reiner: Direct examination by DuPage County Coroner Richard Ballinger, 1982. -- Turner, K L. Coroner's Report for Mary McFarland, September 30, 1982.

8   The coroners' offices in Cook and DuPage Counties, where the deaths occurred: "Drug death probes reopened." *The Daily Herald*, January 13, 1983.

3   Maybe It's the Tylenol

9   Adam Janus's 24-year-old brother: Pienciak, Richard T. "In reaching for relief, cyanide victims found death." *The Register*, October 3, 1982. – Huiras, Robin. "Illinois Nurse Connected Dots in Tylenol Murders." Nurse.com. November 5, 2007. Accessed March 1, 2010. http://news.nurse.com/apps/pbcs.dll/article?AID=2007711050344

9   Theresa called the Arlington Heights: McKinney, Dave. "A tainted drug, 7 lives shattered." Daily Herald, September 27, 1992. -- Sotonoff, Jamie. "Why cyanide deaths might go unsolved." *Daily Herald*, September 29, 2002.

9   Dr. Kim, who had treated: Kim, Thomas. Telephone interview by author, July, 2010.

10   Helen Jensen, the Elk Grove: Beck, Melinda; Hagar, Mary; LaBreque, Ron; Monroe, Sylvester; Prout, Linda. "The Tylenol Scare." *Newsweek*, October 11, 1982.

11   *This has got to be it*: Beck, Melinda; Hagar, Mary; LaBreque, Ron; Monroe, Sylvester; Prout, Linda. "The Tylenol Scare." *Newsweek*, October 11, 1982.

11   Jensen returned to Northwest: O'Donnell, Maureen. "'Listening' Solved Tylenol Killings." Chicago Sun-Times, September 29, 1992. – Burris, Anne. "5 years later, the Tylenol mystery remains." *Daily Herald*, September 30, 1987.

11   Dr. Kim, however, had not: Kim, Thomas. Telephone interview by author, July, 2010.

11   Meanwhile, Philip Cappitelli: Burris. Anne. "A string of coincidences linked Tylenol poisonings." *The Daily Herald*, October 1, 1982.

12   "This is a wild stab": Beck, Melinda; Hagar, Mary; LaBreque, Ron; Monroe, Sylvester; Prout, Linda. "The Tylenol Scare." *Newsweek*, October 11, 1982.

12   Cappitelli's next call: Malcolm, Andrew H. "100 Agents Hunt for Killer in 7 Tylenol." *The New York Times*, October 3, 1982.

12   An Arlington Heights police officer: Kim, Thomas. Telephone interview by author, July, 2010.

12   The local emergency workers: Nenni, Pete; Van Wye, Joann. "5 dead after taking Tylenol capsules filled with cyanide." *The Daily Herald*, October 1, 1982.

13   At Northwest Community Hospital: Kim, Thomas. Telephone interview by author, July, 2010.

13   At about 2 a.m., Dr. Kim: Kim, Thomas. Telephone interview by author, July, 2010.

13   The sun had not: Beck, Melinda; Hagar, Mary; LaBreque, Ron; Monroe, Sylvester; Prout, Linda. "The Tylenol Scare." *Newsweek*, October 11, 1982.

13   "I could smell": Beck, Melinda; Hagar, Mary; LaBreque, Ron; Monroe, Sylvester; Prout, Linda. "The Tylenol Scare." Newsweek, October 11, 1982.

14   The toxicology tests: Nenni, Pete; Van Wye, Joann "5 Die after taking cyanide filled Tylenol." *The Daily Herald*, October 1, 1982.

14   Years later, Richard Keyworth reflected: Comerford, Michael Sean. "Tylenol case 25 years later: Cold case, cold hearts." *Daily Herald*, September 28, 2007.

14   "Our Theresa is gone": Bannon, Tim: "Close-knit family waiting for justice." *The Daily Herald*, October 7, 1982.

4   Guidance of the Credo

17   In 1982, most of the products: Johnson, Robert Wood. "Johnson Talks It Over." 1949.

17   The importance of Chicago: Foster, Larry. Robert Wood Johnson: *The Gentlemen Rebel*. Lillian Press, 1999.

17   "The Credo": Johnson, Robert Wood. "Our Credo." 1943.

17   "The guidance of the credo": James E. Burke, "Ad Council Speech" (delivered on November 16, 1983), p. 6.

18   Burke had challenged the relevance: O'Reilly, Brian. "J&J Is On a Roll." *Fortune*, December 26, 1994.

18   "HBS (Harvard Business School) had": "2003 Alumni Achievement Awards." Harvard Business School website, 2003. Accessed March 5, 2011. http://www.alumni.hbs.edu/awards/2003/burke.html

18   Burke's career at Johnson & Johnson: "James Burke." Reference for Business website. Accessed July 2, 2011. http://www.referenceforbusiness.com/biography/A-E/Burke-James-1925.html

18   According to a friend: Sherman Stratford P. "You're Invited to the CEOs' Ball. *FORTUNE*, January 15, 1990.

18   After just one year with the company: Callahan David. *Kindred Spirits: Harvard Business School's Extraordinary Class of 1949 and How They Transformed American Business*. Hoboken: Wiley, 2002.

18   Less than a year after leaving: Georgescu, Peter. *The Source of Success*. Jossey Bass. San Francisco, 2005.

18   "You're a bachelor": Badaracco, Joseph. *Questions of Character: Illuminating the Heart of Leadership through Literature*. Boston: Harvard Business Press, 2006.

19   "He really gave it to me": Badaracco, Joseph. *Questions of Character: Illuminating the Heart of Leadership through Literature*. Boston: Harvard Business Press, 2006.

19   With a growing list of disappointing: Callahan, David. *Kindred Spirits: Harvard Business School's Extraordinary Class of 1949 and How They Transformed American Business*: Hoboken: Wiley, 2002. -- Georgescu, Peter. The Source of Success. San Francisco: Jossey Bass, 2005.

19   "I thought I was going": O'Reilly, Brian. "J&J Is On a Roll." *Fortune*, December 26, 1994.

19   "Are you the man": Callahan David. *Kindred Spirits: Harvard Business School's Extraordinary Class of 1949 and How They Transformed American Business*: Wiley, 2002

19   Burke moved up: Georgescu, Peter. The Source of Success. San Francisco: Jossey Bass, 2005. -- "James Burke." Reference for Business website, Accessed July 2, 2011. http://www.referenceforbusiness.com/biography/A-E/Burke-James-1925.html   -- Johnson & Johnson. "Johnson & Johnson 1961 Annual Report." 1962

20   In 1975, while Burke: "Johnson & Johnson." *International Directory of Company Histories*, January 1, 1991.

20   In 1978, McNeil Laboratories became: About Tylenol/McNeil. McNeil website. 2011.   Accessed   June   30,   2011. http://www.tylenol.com/page.jhtml?id=tylenol/about/subty.inc

20   A large annual Tylenol advertising budget: Church, George J.; Griggs, Lee; Zagorin, Adam "Murder by Remote Control." *TIME*, October 18, 1982.

5   What Happened in Chicago?

21   Dr. Edmund Donoghue: Associated Press. Pain Capsules Killed Three. *Alton Telegraph*, September 30, 1982.

21   Just prior to Donoghue's press conference: Moore, Thomas. "The Fight to Save Tylenol." *TIME*, November 29, 1982.

21   "Is this about": Moore, Thomas. "The Fight to Save Tylenol." *TIME*, November 29, 1982.

22   Murray's next call went to Arthur Quilty: Moore, Thomas. "The Fight to Save Tylenol." *TIME*, November 29, 1982.

22   The Personal Products Company: "Personal Products Co. plans major expansion." The Circle, June 30, 1971, pg. 9. -- Richards, Cindy. "Johnson & Johnson closing plant." *Chicago Sun-Times*, March 7, 1990.

22   "Are you sure": Moore, Thomas. "The Fight to Save Tylenol." *TIME*, November 29, 1982.

23   "It was a felicitous appointment for me": Moore, Thomas. "The Fight to Save Tylenol." *TIME*, November 29, 1982.

23   Larry Foster, J&J's Vice President: Foster, Lawrence. Interview by PSU students. "Interview with Larry Foster (2002)." -- Foster, Lawrence. "The Tylenol Tragedy: A Crime Without Precedent," in *Communicating in a Healthcare Crisis*, ed. Pines, Wayne L. 173-182, Church Falls: FDAnews, 2007.

23   "That was a bombshell": Cooke, Jeremy R. "PSU alumnus recalls 1982 Tylenol murders." Collegian, October 18, 2002.

23   "I never came home": Cooke, Jeremy R. "PSU alumnus recalls 1982 Tylenol murders." Collegian, October 18, 2002.

23   One-word description of my reaction: Cooke, Jeremy R. "PSU alumnus recalls 1982 Tylenol murders." Collegian, October 18, 2002.

24   Tylenol was bringing in $450 million: Foster, Lawrence. "The Tylenol Tragedy: A Crime Without Precedent," in *Communicating in a Healthcare Crisis*, ed. Pines, Wayne L. 173-182, Church Falls: FDAnews, 2007. -- Moore, Thomas. "The Fight to Save Tylenol." *TIME*, November 29, 1982.

24   Burke immediately focused: David Berg and Stephen Robb. "Crisis Management and the 'Paradigm Case,'" in *Rhetorical and Critical Approaches to Public Relations*, ed. Toth, Elizabeth. Hillsdale: Lawrence Erlbaum Associates, 1992, pg. 92-107. -- Foster, Lawrence. "The Tylenol Tragedy: A Crime Without Precedent," in *Communicating in a Healthcare Crisis*, ed. Pines, Wayne L. 173-182, Church Falls: FDAnews, 2007.

24   Many times, according to Foster: Cooke, Jeremy R. "PSU alumnus recalls 1982 Tylenol murders." Collegian, October 18, 2002 -- Foster, Lawrence. Interview by PSU students, 2002.

24   Burke told David Collins: Fink, Steven. *Crisis Management: Planning for the Inevitable*. American Management Association, 1986, 204-6.

24   "Take charge": Fink, Steven. *Crisis Management: Planning for the Inevitable*. American Management Association: 1986, 204-6.

24   Meanwhile, police cruisers: Tifft, Susan; Lee, Griggs. "Poison Madness in the Midwest." *TIME*, October 11, 1982.

25   Initially, Johnson & Johnson did not: Beck, Melinda, Mary Hagar, Ron LaBreque, Sylvester Monroe, Linda Prout. "The Tylenol Scare." *Newsweek*. October 11, 1982.

25   "We currently have no evidence": Cunningham, Kathy. "Local Tylenol Distributor Sure of Safety." *The Winchester Star*, October 2, 1982.

6 J&J Takes Charge

27 Ninety minutes after James Burke: Moore, Thomas. "The Fight to Save Tylenol." *TIME*, November 29, 1982.

27 "I needed my own": Moore, Thomas. "The Fight to Save Tylenol." *TIME*, November 29, 1982.

27 Collins also called another: "New Hall of Fame Members." Fenwick Magazine, spring 2003, 12.

27 "a place to build": "New Hall of Fame Members." Fenwick Magazine, spring 2003, 12.

28 "putting a state, indeed a nation, into fear": UPI. "Laced Tylenol claims 7th; culprit unknown," Pacific Stars and Stripes, October 4, 1982.

28 Illinois Governor Jim Thompson: "Northwestern Grants Degrees to 39 Villagers," *Oak Leaves*, July 2, 1959. -- James R. Thompson. Winston & Strawn website. Accessed July 2, 2011. http://www.winston.com/index.cfm?contentID=24&itemID=10873

28 Governor Thompson put Tyrone Fahner: Associated Press. "Fahner will lead Tylenol probe." Chronicle-Telegram, October 4, 1982. – Lee, Thomas J. "Tylenol case easing Fanner's ills." *The Daily Herald*, October 5, 1982.

28 But that anonymity changed instantly: Hughes, T Lee. "Tylenol Capsules Change Course of Illinois race." *Chillicothe Constitution-Tribune*, October 28, 1982.

28 A *Chicago Tribune* Poll released October 2, 1982: Man in the News: Sheppard, Nathaniel. "Anonymous Investigator." *New York Times*, October 5, 1982.

28 One of Fahner's first official acts: "Tylenol murders last year recalled." *Nightly News*. NBC, September 28, 1983.

28 Chicago police officers were advised: ABC Eyewitness News. ABC, WLS-TV, Chicago, September 30, 1982.

28 "may be contaminated with cyanide, and should be destroyed": ABC *Eyewitness News*. ABC, WLS-TV, Chicago, September 30, 1982.

29 Larry Foster said there were about 150 or 175 calls: Foster, Lawrence. Interview by PSU students, 2002. http://instruct.tri-c.edu/jkerezy/Larry_Foster_Video_Interview.pdf

29 "We were clean": Nenni, Pete; Van Wye, Joann "5 Die after taking cyanide filled Tylenol." *The Daily Herald*, October 1, 1982.

29 One day later J&J was forced to retract: Foster, Lawrence, interview by PSU students. Interview with Larry Foster: 2002 -- Fearn-Banks, Kathleen. "Case: Johnson & Johnson and the Tylenol Murders," in *Crisis communications: A Casebook Approach*. Mahwah: Lawrence Erlbaum Associates, 1996, 86-96.

29 McNeil President, Joseph Chiesa, received: Moore, Thomas. "The Fight to Save Tylenol." *TIME*, November 29, 1982.

30 A two-way video: Foster, Lawrence. "The Tylenol Tragedy: A Crime Without Precedent," in *Communicating in a Healthcare Crisis*, ed. Pines, Wayne L. 173-182, Church Falls: FDAnews, 2007.

30   Twenty-five public relations employees from other J&J operating companies: David Berg and Stephen Robb. "Crisis Management and the 'Paradigm Case,'" in *Rhetorical and Critical Approaches to Public Relations*, ed. Toth, Elizabeth. Hillsdale: Lawrence Erlbaum Associates, 1992, pg. 92-107.

30   Public relations personnel: Foster, Lawrence. "The Tylenol Tragedy: A Crime Without Precedent," in *Communicating in a Healthcare Crisis*, ed. Pines, Wayne L. 173-182, Church Falls: FDAnews, 2007.

31   Andrews, along with: David Berg and Stephen Robb. "Crisis Management and the 'Paradigm Case,'" in *Rhetorical and Critical Approaches to Public Relations*, ed. Toth, Elizabeth. Hillsdale: Lawrence Erlbaum Associates, 1992, pg. 92-107. – Fearn-Banks, Kathleen. "Case: Johnson & Johnson and the Tylenol Murders," in *Crisis communications: A Casebook Approach*. Mahwah: Lawrence Erlbaum Associates, 1996, 86-96.

31   "collectively shocked": Fearn-Banks, Kathleen. "Case: Johnson & Johnson and the Tylenol Murders," in *Crisis communications: A Casebook Approach*. Mahwah: Lawrence Erlbaum Associates, 1996, 86-96.

7   The Hospital

33   The autopsy of Lynn Reiner: Coroner's inquest, re: Lynn Reiner. Direct examination by DuPage County Coroner Richard Ballinger, 1982.

33   "retrieve any and all bottles of Tylenol": Coroner's inquest, re: Lynn Reiner. Direct examination by DuPage County Coroner Richard Ballinger, 1982.

33   At around 11:00 a.m.: Coroner's inquest, re: Lynn Reiner. Direct examination by DuPage County Coroner Richard Ballinger, 1982. -- Reiner, Ed. Personal interview by author. Winfield, IL, May 22, 2010.

34   After Sostak and Watkins finished: Coroner's inquest, re: Lynn Reiner. Direct examination by DuPage County Coroner Richard Ballinger, 1982. -- Pirl, Joerge. Telephone interview by author, 2010. -- Siekmann, Peter. DuPage County Coroner's Office Preliminary Report, re: Mary Reiner, September 30, 1982.

34   Siekmann said that shortly before: Associated Press. "Poison Tylenol Kills Five." The Capital, October 1, 1982. -- Duerksen, Susan. "6th poison victim dies; 2 more believed linked with Tylenol." *The Daily Herald*, October 1, 1982.

34   Siekmann said the lot number: Associated Press. "Poison Tylenol Kills Five." The Capital, October 1, 1982. -- Duerksen, Susan. "6th poison victim dies; 2 more believed linked with Tylenol." *The Daily Herald*, October 1, 1982.

35   In fact, 90 percent: Boatright, John R. Ethics and the Conduct of Business. Prentice Hall, 2002.

35   Central DuPage Hospital had converted: Central DuPage Hospital. "Key Milestones in Our History." CDH.org. http://www.cdh.org/About-Us/Our-History.aspx

35   The American Society of Hospital: American Society of Hospital Pharmacists. "ASHP technical assistance bulletin on hospital drug distribution and control." Am J Hosp Pharm., 1980.

35   Inpatient self-care and "discharge" medications: American Society of Hospital Pharmacists. "ASHP technical assistance bulletin on hospital drug distribution and control." Am J Hosp Pharm., 1980.

36   By Thursday afternoon, J&J had assigned Chicago area sales reps: Associated Press. "Poisoned Tylenol kills 5." *The Capital*, October 1, 1982.

36   The capsules from those outlets were never inspected: Griffin, Leslie. "One year later: Tylenol, Trauma recedes, search for killer goes on." The Stars and Stripes, August 21, 1983.

36   Late Thursday morning, the pathologist: Turner, K L. Coroner's Report for Mary McFarland, September 30, 1982.

36   Lombard police went to Mary's: Turner, K L. Coroner's Report for Mary McFarland, September 30, 1982. -- McFadden, Robert D. "Poison Deaths Bring U.S. Warning on Tylenol Use." *The New York Times*, October 2, 1982.

36   Lombard Police Detectives visited: Turner, K L. Coroner's Report: Mary McFarland, September 30, 1982.

37   The deaths of Mary McFarland and: Moore, Thomas. "The Fight to Save Tylenol." TIME, November 29, 1982. -- Duerksen, Susan. "6th poison victim dies; 2 more believed linked with Tylenol." *The Daily Herald*, October 1, 1982.

37   J&J said the recall consisted of 93,000: Associated Press. "Stockbroker may have been victim in extortion letter hoax." *The News*, October 9, 1982.

37   J&J spokesperson Robert Kniffin said the batch went directly: Associated Press, "Poison pills take 5 lives, cause panic," *Herald-Zeitung*, October 1, 1982.

37   These J&J distribution centers were referenced in a 1983 Harvard: Aguilar, Francis J.; Bhambri, Arvind. "Johnson & Johnson (B) Hospital Services." Harvard Business School Publishing, June 30, 1986.

37   Robert Kniffin said in February: McFadden, Robert D. "Two Bottles of Poisoned Tylenol Were Shipped By Same Distributor." *New York Times*, February 16, 1986.

38   In the 1970s and 1980s, the DOD: DOD Contract with McNeil Consumer Products Company, Fort Washington, Pennsylvania. Contract number DLA12083C0127, January 1983. --- DOD Contract with McNeil Consumer Products Company, Fort Washington, Pennsylvania. Contract number DLA12083C0677, September 1983. --- DOD Contract with McNeil Consumer Products Company, Round Rock, Texas, Contract number LA12082 C0776, May 1982. --- DOD (Air force) Contract with McNeil Consumer Products Co., Glendale, CA. Contract number SA13H 77 50158, Fiscal year 1980.

38   News of what became: Tifft, Susan; Lee, Griggs. "Poison Madness in the Midwest." *TIME*, October 11, 1982. – Foster, Lawrence. "The Tylenol Tragedy: A Crime Without Precedent," in *Communicating in a Healthcare Crisis*, ed. Pines, Wayne L. 173-182, Church Falls: FDAnews, 2007.

38   "I don't think": Kleinfield, N.R. "Long, Uphill Odds for Tylenol." New York Times, October 8, 1982.

39   After a long day at McNeil: Moore, Thomas. "The Fight to Save Tylenol." *TIME*, November 29, 1982.

39   The Tylenol in McFarland's bottle: McFadden, Robert D. "Poison Deaths Bring U.S. Warning on Tylenol Use." *The New York Times*; October 2, 1982 -- Rutenberg, Sharon. "Five poison deaths prompt." *The Hawk Eye*, October 1, 1982.

39   "The fact that": Moore, Thomas. "The Fight to Save Tylenol." *TIME*, November 29, 1982.

40   Larry Foster and J&J spokesperson, Marshall Malloy: Rutenberg, Sharon. "Five poison deaths prompt." *The Hawk Eye*, October 1, 1982.: David Berg and Stephen Robb. "Crisis Management and the 'Paradigm Case,'" in *Rhetorical and Critical Approaches to Public Relations*, ed. Toth, Elizabeth. Hillsdale: Lawrence Erlbaum Associates, 1992, pg. 92-107. -- Associated Press, "More poison is found in Tylenol Pills." *The Chronicle-Telegram*, October 1, 1982.

40   "They [McNeil] checked us three times: Montgomery, Jeff. "Tylenol Removed From Area Stores." *Altoona Mirror*, October 2, 1982.

40   "I think they": Montgomery, Jeff. "Tylenol Removed From Area Stores." *Altoona Mirror*, October 2, 1982.

40   "leads us to believe strongly": Associated Press. "'Madman' sought in poisonings." *Wisconsin State Journal*, October 2, 1982.

41   "We naturally wanted": Cooke, Jeremy R. "PSU alumnus recalls 1982 Tylenol murders." *Collegian*, October 18, 2002.

41   Though Collins said he didn't know: Moore, Thomas. "The Fight to Save Tylenol." *TIME*, November 29, 1982.

41   The lot number on the label: Code of Federal Regulations Title 21, Section 201.18.

41   J&J had now recalled 264,000 bottles: McFadden, Robert D. "Poison Deaths Bring U.S. Warning on Tylenol Use." *The New York Times*, October 2, 1982.

42   The public was just learning: Associated Press. "Madman sought in cyanide deaths." *Lethbridge Herald*, October 2, 1982.

42   Paula had the following: Pienciak, Richard T. "In reaching for relief, cyanide victims found death." *The Register*, October 3, 1982. -- United Press International. "Laced Tylenol claims 7th; culprit unknown." *Pacific Stars and Stripes*, October 4, 1982.

42   Later, while viewing video footage from a security camera: Associated Press. "Tylenol case photo clue 'significant'." *The Paris New*, October 19, 1982.

42   Chicago Police Superintendant: Associated Press. "Madman sought in cyanide deaths." *Lethbridge Herald*, October 2, 1982.

42   The Tylenol in Prince's bottle was from Lot 1801MA: Associated Press. "Byrne bans sale of all Tylenol in the big city." *Sunday Roswell Daily Record*, October 3, 1982.

42   Chicago Mayor Jane Byrne held: Wolohan, Linda. "Poisoned Pills kill at Least Six Persons." *The Progress*, October 2, 1982.

43   The FDA had released: Associated Press. "Tylenol spiked with cyanide blamed for five deaths." The *Lethbridge Herald*, October 1, 1982.

43   The FDA had also informed consumers: "Tylenol Contamination." *Nightline*. ABC, October 1, 1982.

43   Standard FDA inspections: FDA 483 Inspection Observations: McNeil Consumer Products Co., Fort Washington, PA, December 9, 2010. -- FDA 483 Inspection Observations: McNeil Consumer Products Co., Las Piedras, PR, November 2, 2010.

43   In a report to the U.S. Congress: Government Accountability Office. "FDA's Approach to Reviewing Over-The-Counter Drugs is Reasonable, But Progress is Slow." GAO Report, April 26, 1982.

43   Incredibly,   up   until   1997:   Government   Accountability   Office. "NONPRESCRIPTION DRUGS: Over the Counter and Underemphasized," GAO Report, January 10, 1992.

43   After 1991 investigation of the FDA's procedures: Government Accountability Office. "Non-Prescription Drugs: Over the Counter and Underemphasized." GAO Report, January 10, 1992.

44   The existence of these complaints was not disclosed until 1991: Janota, Laura. "Fear of negative publicity likely led to Tylenol settlement." *The Daily Herald*, May 15, 1991.

44   "Either capsules were missing, or some other medication was mixed in or there were foreign objects": Associated Press. "Families of poisoning victims can sue Tylenol, judge rules." *Syracuse Herald-Journal*, September 13, 1990.

9   Rational Evildoer

45   According to the stories widely: Beck, Melinda; Hagar, Mary; LaBreque, Ron; Monroe, Sylvester; Prout, Linda. "The Tylenol Scare." *Newsweek*, October 11, 1982. – Associated Press. "Cyanide Madman Sought." *The Titusville Herald*, October 2, 1982. -- Associated Press. "Sixth Victim Claimed By Cyanide Pills." *Bedford Gazette*, October 2, 1982.

45   We believe it [the tamperings] happened: Nenni, Pete; Van Wye, Joann "5 Die after taking cyanide filled Tylenol." *The Daily Herald*, October 1, 1982.

45   Jim Adamson, a spokesperson: United Press International. "Kansans told not to use Tylenol." *Salina Journal*, October 3, 1982.

45   "We're investigating stereotypes": Cohen, Sharon. "Investigators Hunt for Madman in Tylenol Case." *Chillicothe Constitution-Tribune*, October 2, 1982.

45   In the following days: Malcolm, Andrew H. "Search for the Tylenol Killer: Many Clues, But No Solution." *New York Times*, October 10, 1982.

45   Fahner laid out the basic premise: Associated Press. "Tylenol Investigation Continues." Bedford Gazette, October 4, 1982.

45   Fahner said the potassium cyanide: Malcolm, Andrew H. "100 Agents Hunt for Killer in 7 Tylenol Deaths." *The New York Times*, October 3, 1982.

46   Cook County Medical Examiner: Associated Press. "Suspects Studied in Cyanide Deaths." *Casa Grande Dispatch*, October 4, 1982.

46   "We're at 48 hours now": Litke, James. "Cyanide kills Philadelphian." *The Gettysburg Times*, October 7, 1982.

49   *The Daily Herald* reported: Madrzyk, Anna; Gores, Paul. "Cyanide Killer Search Widens." *The Sunday Herald*, October 3, 1982.

49   *The New York Times* also reported: Malcolm, Andrew H. "Search for the Tylenol Killer: Many Clues, But No Solution." *New York Times*, October 10, 1982.

49   Fahner said these bottles would be "particularly helpful": Madrzyk, Anna; Gores, Paul. "Cyanide Killer Search Widens." *The Sunday Herald*, October 3, 1982.

49   Later that night, an FDA: Associated Press. "7th Chicago-area death blamed on poisoned drug." The News, October 2, 1982.

49   On Saturday, the story changed a little more: Associated Press. "Madman's Plot Suspected; More Tainted Tylenol Found." *The News Record*, October 2, 1982. -- Litke, James; Associated Press. "Poisoning done in killer's home." *The Gettysburg Times*, October 4, 1982.

49   "Two more poisoned containers": Novitch, Mark, "Tylenol: The Granddady of Crisis," in *Communicating in a Healthcare Crisis*, ed. Pines, Wayne L. 183-186, Church Falls: FDAnews, 2007.

50   "We don't know": Doyle, Pat. "A year after Tylenol killings: sorrow lingers, answers elude." The Sunday Herald, September 25, 1983.

50   One year after the Tylenol murders: *Evening News*, NBC: September 28, 1983.

50   A survey conducted by Audits and Surveys: Zdep, Stanley M.; Roshwalb, Irving. "The Affects of the Tylenol Poisonings on Consumer Fears." Audits and Surveys Inc., 1982.

50   Video clips taken: *Nightly News*. NBC, October 8, 1982.

50   Fahner said only one contaminated bottle: Malcolm, Andrew. "Capsule Deaths: A hunt for more than one suspect," *New York Times*, October 4, 1982. -- Dowling, John. "Leads 'substantial' in the Tylenol case." *Syracuse Herald Journal*, October 4, 1982.

51   "The media did": Duerksen, Susan. "Last 2 families of Tylenol dead file damage suits." *The Daily Herald*, June 2, 1983.

51   "We're still in the process": United Press International. "'Not Close' To Arrest: Tylenol Case Stumps Authorities." *Tyrone Daily Herald*, October 8, 1982.

51   "rational evil doer": United Press International. "Tylenol poisoning probe narrowed to 4 suspects." *Pacific Stars and Stripes*, October 11, 1982.

10   A Cooperative Effort

53   Under Title 21 of the U.S. Code of Federal Regulations: CFR Title 21 PART 211

53   Richard Epstein, a law professor: Bannon, Tim. "'McNeil may not be liable'." The Sunday Herald, October 3, 1982.

54   "One of the things": Moore, Thomas. "The Fight to Save Tylenol." *TIME*, November 29, 1982.

54   Douglas, according to the biography on his web site: John Douglas Mindhunter website. Accessed July 1, 2011 http://www.johndouglasmindhunter.com/home.php

54   "Despite the fact": Douglas, John. Mind Hunter. New York: Pocket Books, 2000.

54   "The country was": Douglas, John. Mind Hunter. New York: Pocket Books, 2000.

54   Dawn Hobbs, a journalist: Bell, Rachael. The Tylenol Terrorist. 2011 http://www.trutv.com/library/crime/terrorists_spies/terrorists/tylenol_murders/3.html

55   "The public was served": "Letter to the Stockholders," in Johnson & Johnson's 1982 Annual Report, 1983.

55   "A demonstration without parallel": Foster, Lawrence. "The Tylenol Tragedy: A Crime Without Precedent," in Communicating in a Healthcare Crisis, ed. Pines, Wayne L. 173-182, Church Falls: FDAnews, 2007.

55   Johnson & Johnson established: Kaplan, Tamara. "The Tylenol Crisis: How Effective Public Relations Saved Johnson & Johnson." Pennsylvania State University: November 2003

55   In this way, according to a public relations executive: Kaplan, Tamara. "The Tylenol Crisis: How Effective Public Relations Saved Johnson & Johnson." Pennsylvania State University, November 2003.

55   Larry Foster said J&J talked: Foster, Lawrence. "The Tylenol Tragedy: A Crime Without Precedent," in Communicating in a Healthcare Crisis, ed. Pines, Wayne L. 173-182, Church Falls: FDAnews, 2007.

55   Johnson & Johnson: strengthened its ties with the FBI: United Press International. "Trucker's Death Probed; List of Suspects Reduced." Altoona Mirror, October 6, 1982.

56   J&J has routinely hired: Bloomberg. "China Counterfeit Diabetes Tests Tracked by J&J." Bloomberg website, August 16, 2007. Accessed July 7, 2011. -- http://www.bloomberg.com/apps/news?pid=newsarchive&sid=aCAuLKG2YwKc . - Hubbard, William K. "Importation of Prescription Drugs." FDA website, July 14, 2001. Accessed   July   7,   2011.   -- http://www.fda.gov/newsevents/testimony/ucm113655.htm . -- Eban, Katherine, "Drug theft goes big." CNN website, March 31, 2011. Accessed July 7, 2011.

56   "Bob Andrews spent":   Foster, Lawrence. Interview by PSU students, 2002.

57   That lab, staffed with 30 J&J toxicologists: ABC-News. ABC, October 1, 1982 – United Press International. "Authorities Expand Tylenol Search." *Altoona Mirror*, October 2, 1982.

57   On Friday, just the second day: Duerksin, Susan. "6th poison victim dies; 2 more believed linked with Tylenol." *The Daily Herald*, October 2, 1982.

11   Handling the Evidence

59   Chicago Mayor, Jane Byrne: David Berg and Stephen Robb. "Crisis Management and the 'Paradigm Case,'" in *Rhetorical and Critical Approaches to Public Relations*, ed. Toth, Elizabeth. Hillsdale: Lawrence Erlbaum Associates, 1992, pg. 92-107. -- AP. "Chicago's Mayor bans Tylenol sales," *The Register*, October 3, 1982

59   Two days earlier: David Berg and Stephen Robb. "Crisis Management and the 'Paradigm Case,'" in *Rhetorical and Critical Approaches to Public Relations*, ed. Toth, Elizabeth. Hillsdale: Lawrence Erlbaum Associates, 1992, pg. 92-107.

59   J&J's local attorney, Paul Noland: David Berg and Stephen Robb. "Crisis Management and the 'Paradigm Case,'" in *Rhetorical and Critical Approaches to Public Relations*, ed. Toth, Elizabeth. Hillsdale: Lawrence Erlbaum Associates, 1992, pg. 92-107.

60   The Food and Drug Administration, the investigative authorities: Gates, Thomas N. "McNeil Consumer Products Co. 'Dear Doctor' Letter": signed by Dr. Thomas N. Gates, October 13, 1982.

60   FDA Deputy Commissioner, Mark Novitch, said: Associated Press. "Tylenol task force being cut back." The Chronicle-Telegram: November 9, 1982 -- New York Times News Service. "Over-counter drug safety is a priority." *Wisconsin State Journal*, October 6, 1982.

60   The *New York Times* reported: "Cyanide is Discovered in Tylenol in an April Death in Philadelphia." *The New York Times*, October 7, 1982.

60   A United Press International story: United Press International. "Another Cyanide Death Prevented." Altoona Mirror, October 22, 1982.

60   There were about 165,000 outlets nationwide: Reis, Al; Trout, Jack. Marketing Warfare. New York: The McGraw Hill Companies, 2006, Pg. 62.

60   About 11,000 were in the Chicago area: Beck, Melinda, Mary Hagar, Ron LaBreque, Sylvester Monroe, Linda Prout. "The Tylenol Scare." *Newsweek*, October 11, 1982.

60   By late Saturday afternoon: Madrzyk, Anna; Gores, Paul. "Cyanide Killer Search Widens." *The Sunday Herald*: October 3, 1982.

61   "We're trying to": Dowling, John. "Leads 'substantial' in the Tylenol case." *Syracuse Herald Journal*, October 4, 1982.

61   "They range in age from a young hippie": C Malcolm, Andrew. "Capsule Deaths: A hunt for more than one suspect," *New York Times*, October 4, 1982.

61   The suspects at the top: "Chicago lie tests clear 6." *Chicago Sun Times*, October 27, 1982. – Coroner's inquest, re: Mary McFarland. Direct examination by DuPage County Coroner Richard Ballinger, December 14, 1982.

62   Authorities also could have: Houston, Jack. "Local Firm Helps Put Tylenol to The Test." *Chicago Tribune*, February 23, 1986.

63   "No human hands touched the Tylenol or its ingredients": Janson, Donald. "Maker of Tylenol Cleared of Blame." *The New York Times*, October 6, 1982.

12   Rack Jobbers

65   The *Daily News Record* reported: Dulan, Tom. "Suspect Tylenol Found Here." *Daily News Record*, October 2, 1982.

65   "Sav-A-Stop," a nationally: Dulan, Tom. "Suspect Tylenol Found Here." Daily News Record, October 2, 1982.

65   Rack jobbers are wholesale distribution: FTC Complaint. In the Matter of Sterling Drug: Order and Opinion Etc, in regard to the alleged violation of section 7 of the Clayton Act 1972.

66   Ann Saylor, the manager: "2nd IGA Finds Suspect Tylenol." Daily News Record, October 4, 1982.

66   The general manager of Sav-A-Stop: Dulan, Tom. "Suspect Tylenol Found Here." Daily News Record, October 2, 1982.

66   Spokespersons for Kroger and Safeway: Dulan, Tom. "Suspect Tylenol Found Here." Daily News Record, October 2, 1982.

66   Safeway and Kroger, the two largest supermarket: Morris, John; Ringer, Richard. "K mart joins financial services race: announcement today planned by retailer." American Banker: January 12, 1984 -- Weinstein, Michael. "Supermarket chain, Bethesda bank in venture to operate ATM system." American Banker, January 26, 1984.

66   According to *Newsweek*, many experts: Beck, Melinda, Mary Hagar, Ron LaBreque, Sylvester Monroe, Linda Prout. "The Tylenol Scare." Newsweek, October 11, 1982.

67   FDA Deputy Commissioner, Mark Novitch, said: Associated Press. "Cyanide Madman Sought." The Titusville Herald, October 2, 1982.

67   Sav-A-Stop, a privately held: Key, Janet. "Brennan Going Back To Wards As Chief Exec." Chicago Tribune, May 04, 1985.

67   For: Rack jobbing services: U.S Patent 802,008, registered January 11, 1966.

67   The nation's leading non-food: Sav-A-Stop. "Stock Merchandisers." The Daily Herald, July 30, 1982.

68   Officials surmised that: The Tylenol Murders. Kowalski, W.J. 2011 http://www.aerobiologicalengineering.com/wxk116/TylenolMurders/ -- Associated Press. "Tylenol Investigation Continues." Bedford Gazette, October 4, 1982.

68   J&J spokesperson Robert Kniffin said: Associated Press. "Stockbroker may have been victim in extortion letter hoax." *The News*, October 9, 1982.

68   But after a second Tylenol tampering incident: Prokesch, Steven, "Tylenol Capsule Output is Suspended by Maker." *New York Times*, February 14, 1986.

69   Annual Tylenol sales were about $450 million: Foster, Lawrence. "The Tylenol Tragedy: A Crime Without Precedent," in *Communicating in a Healthcare Crisis*, ed. Pines, Wayne L. 173-182, Church Falls: FDAnews, 2007. -- Moore, Thomas. "The Fight to Save Tylenol." *TIME*, November 29, 1982. -- Kerr, Peter Tylenol is Linked to a Cyanide Death in Yonkers." *The New York Times*, February 11, 1986.

69   About 30 percent of those sales were from capsules: McFadden, Robert D. "Maker of Tylenol Discontinuing All Over-The-Counter Drug Capsule." The New York Times, February 18, 1986.

69   Pharmaceutical wholesalers typically carry: "Wholesale Inventory Turn Data." Strategosinc website, Accessed July 11, 2011. http://www.strategosinc.com/articles/warehouse_inventory_turns.htm

69   Food and drug stores also: "Wholesale Inventory Turn Data." Strategosinc website, Accessed July 11, 2011. http://www.strategosinc.com/articles/warehouse_inventory_turns.htm -- Matyjewicz, George. "Inventory Turns." Business know-how website. Accessed June 11, 2011. http://www.businessknowhow.com/manage/inventory.htm

69   An "FDA Alert" regarding a shipment of bulk Tylenol: FDA. "FDA Witnesses Destruction of Drug Products." FDA website. June 28, 2001. Accessed July 1, 2011. http://www.fda.gov/ICECI/EnforcementActions/EnforcementStory/EnforcementSto ryArchive/ucm107058.htm

13   A Reluctant Recall

71   Sergeant David Burrows: Associated Press. "Officials report some leads in cyanide case." *The Paris News*, October 4, 1982.

71   The boxes "said Tylenol": Associated Press. "Officials report some leads in cyanide case." *The Paris News*, October 4, 1982.

76   "It looked like hundreds of capsules": Malcolm, Andrew H. "Cyanide Case Focuses on Find in Parking Lot at All-night Restaurant." *The New York Times*, October 5, 1982.

71   "We just blew it off": Wolfe, John. "'We should have known.'" *Pacific Stars and Stripes*, October 12, 1982.

72   "It was evident they": Associated Press. "Officials report some leads in cyanide case." *The Paris News*, October 4, 1982.

72   "The symptoms reported": Associated Press. "Officials report some leads in cyanide case." *The Paris News*, October 4, 1982.

72   "I was stupid": Wolfe, John. "'We should have known.'" *Pacific Stars and Stripes*, October 12, 1982.

72   FBI agents were seen questioning: Malcolm, Andrew H. "Cyanide Case Focuses on Find in Parking Lot at All-night Restaurant." *The New York Times*, October 5, 1982.

72   "I wish you guys": Gores, Paul. "Poisonings draw top coverage." *The Daily Herald*, October 7, 1982.

72   While FBI agents were questioning: Fannin, Rebecca. "Tylenol: diary of an amazing comeback." *TIME*, March 22, 1983. – Georgescu, Peter. *The Source of Success.* San Francisco: Jossey Bass, 2005.

72   J&J President David Clare said the climate within: Solomon, Robert C. *It's good business: ethics and free enterprise for the new millennium.* Rowman & Littlefield Publishers Inc. 1997, p168-169.

73   For a period of about 48: Solomon, Robert C. *It's good business: ethics and free enterprise for the new millennium.* Rowman & Littlefield Publishers Inc., 1997, p168-169.

73   Burke and Nelson were in their second day: Church, George J.; Griggs, Lee; Zagorin, Adam "Murder by Remote Control." *TIME*, October 18, 1982.

73   His wife, Terry: Dowling, John. "Strychnine-laced Tylenol found in California." *The Sequin Gazette-Enterprise*, October 6, 1982.

74   Dr. Clay called Johnson & Johnson: Associated Press. "Strychnine-tainted Tylenol found". *Galveston Daily News*, October 8, 1982.

74   As it turned out: Church, George J.; Griggs, Lee; Zagorin, Adam "Murder by Remote Control." *TIME*, October 18, 1982. -- Associated Press. "Tylenol victim quizzed by lie detector test." *Gazette*, October 14, 1982.

74   The FBI officially closed the Oroville: Associated Press. "Probe of 'copycat' Tylenol case ends." *The Register*, November 27, 1982.

74   When the Oroville tampering incident: Dowling, John. "Strychnine-laced Tylenol found in California." *The Sequin Gazette-Enterprise*, October 6, 1982.

75   "The FBI didn't want us to do it":   Moore, Thomas. "The Fight to Save Tylenol." *TIME*, November 29, 1982.

75   Burke's suggestion that he: "Tylenol's "Miracle" Comeback: A year after the poisonings, public confidence is restored." *TIME*, October 17, 1983 -- David Berg and Stephen Robb. "Crisis Management and the 'Paradigm Case,'" in *Rhetorical and Critical Approaches to Public Relations*, ed. Toth, Elizabeth. Hillsdale: Lawrence Erlbaum Associates, 1992, pg. 92-107.

75   Police had said that Lynn Reiner's: Associated Press. "Search pressed for clues in poisonings." *The Frederick Post*, October 4, 1982.

75   The cyanide-laced Tylenol that killed Paula Prince: Associated Press. "Byrne bans sale of all Tylenol in the big city." *Sunday Roswell Daily Record*, October 3, 1982.

75   Authorities had also found cyanide in Tylenol capsules: Duerksen, Susan. "6th poison victim dies; 2 more believed linked with Tylenol." *The Daily Herald*, October 1, 1982.

75   Strychnine-laced Tylenol capsules from yet another lot: Dowling, John. "Strychnine-laced Tylenol found in California." *The Sequin Gazette-Enterprise*, October 6, 1982.

75   By the end of the second day of the investigation, authorities had recovered poisoned Tylenol capsules from seven different lots: Associated Press. "Tylenol Investigation Continues." *Bedford Gazette*, October 4, 1982.

75   "In conjunction with":   United Press International. "Over the Counter Pill Sales Dropping." *The Progress*, October 6, 1982.

76   "The confidence of":   Associated Press. "Contaminated Tylenol case may cost maker $75 million." *Waterloo Courier*, October 7, 1982.

76   "Plaintiff (J&J) itself admits":   McNeilab, Inc., Plaintiff v. North River Insurance Co. et al., Defendants, 645 F. Supp. 525, 543-45 (D.N.J.), September 17, 1986.

76   The transcript in McNeilab Inc.:   McNeilab, Inc., Plaintiff v. North River Insurance Co. et al., Defendants, 645 F. Supp. 525, 543-45 (D.N.J.), September 17, 1986.

76   "[McNeil] and its parent (J&J): McNeilab Inc.: McNeilab, Inc., Plaintiff v. North River Insurance Co. et al., Defendants, 645 F. Supp. 525, 543-45 (D.N.J.), September 17, 1986.

77   The mailgrams that J&J faxed to retailers: Cunningham, Kathy. "Local Tylenol Distributor Sure of Safety." *Winchester Star*, October 2, 1982.

77   When Chicago Mayor: David Berg and Stephen Robb. "Crisis Management and the 'Paradigm Case,'" in *Rhetorical and Critical Approaches to Public Relations*, ed. Toth, Elizabeth. Hillsdale: Lawrence Erlbaum Associates, 1992, pg. 92-107.

77   "temporarily suspended production": United Press International. "Tylenol Production Is Halted." *Pharos-Tribune*, October 5, 1982.

77   "There is widespread": Gates, Thomas N. "McNeil Consumer Products Co. 'Dear Doctor' Letter": signed by Dr. Thomas N. Gates, October 13, 1982.

67   J&J executives had learned: Duerksen, Susan. "6th poison victim dies; 2 more believed linked with Tylenol." *The Daily Herald*, October 1, 1982.

14   Vanishing Lot Numbers

79   The task force is asking: 10 p.m. News. WMAQ-TV, NBC, October 1, 1982. -- Duerksen, Susan. "6th poison victim dies; 2 more believed linked with Tylenol." *The Daily Herald*, October 2, 1982.

80   The local Arlington Heights newspaper: Madrzyk, Anna; Gores, Paul. "Cyanide Killer Search Widens." *The Sunday Herald*, October 3, 1982.

80   Late Friday night, shortly before midnight: Wolohan, Linda. "Poisoned Pills kill at Least Six Persons." *The Progress*, October 2, 1982.

80   The poisoned Tylenol that killed Mary McFarland: Associated Press. "Poison Found in Another Tylenol Batch." *Winchester Star*, October 1, 1982.

80   And the cyanide-laced Tylenol that killed Paula Prince: Associated Press. "Byrne bans sale of all Tylenol in the big city." *Sunday Roswell Daily Record*, October 3, 1982.

81   On Saturday, October 2nd, lot numbers 1665LM and MC2884: Associated Press. "7th Chicago-area death blamed on poisoned drug." *The News*, October 2, 1982.

81   The danger list now included only lot numbers MC2880, 1910MD, and 1801MA: Madrzyk, Anna; Gores, Paul. "Cyanide Killer Search Widens." *The Sunday Herald*, October 3, 1982.

81   On Sunday, October 3rd, police: Associated Press. "Search pressed for clues in poisonings." *The Frederick Post*, October 4, 1982.

81   "one bottle labeled Regular Strength Tylenol, Lot 1833MB": Siekmann, Peter. DuPage County Coroner's Office Preliminary Report, re: Mary Reiner, September 30, 1982.

81   Police explained that there had been: Associated Press. "Police Seek Drug Killer." *Daily News Record*, October 4, 1982.

81   Winfield Police Officer Scott Watkins: Watkins, Scott. Personal interview by author, August 19, 2010.

82   "I don't know": Watkins, Scott. Personal interview by author, August 19, 2010.

82   Watkins also said that on Thursday morning: Coroner's inquest, re: Lynn Reiner. Direct examination by DuPage County Coroner Richard Ballinger, 1982. -- Siekman, Peter. DuPage County Coroner's Office Preliminary Report, re: Mary Reiner, September 30, 1982. -- Watkins, Scott. Personal interview by Michelle Rosen, March 12, 2010.

15   Zahn Drug

83   When Central DuPage Hospital converted: Central DuPage Hospital. "Key Milestones in Our History." CDH.org. http://www.cdh.org/About-Us/Our-History.aspx

83   On October 1, 1982, ABC-News: *World News Tonight*. ABC, October 6, 1982. -- Madrzyk, Anna; Gores, Paul. "Cyanide Killer Search Widens." *The Sunday Herald*, October 3, 1982. -- ABC Nightline, ABC, October 1, 1982.

83   Louis Zahn founded: "Louis Zahn dead at 67." *The World*, August 28, 1977.

84   Zahn Drug, with $200 million: "The Wall Street Transcript." The Wall Street Transcript website, May 14, 2001. Accessed July 10, 2011. http://www.twst.com/pdf/visiontek.pdf

84   The company maintained its own delivery operation: Chicago Truck Drivers, Helpers and Warehouse Workers Union Pension Fund, and Paul Glover v. Louis Zahn Drug Co. 88-2498. U.S. Court of Appeals, 7th Circuit, December 11, 1989.

84   The company's headquarters: "Help Wanted, Customer Service." *The Daily Herald*, July 18, 1982.

84   In 1982, Zahn Drug operated a state-of-the-art: Angell, William M. "Material Handling Classics." Small Parts Orderpicking, 1980 Automated Material Handling Storage Systems Conference. Clay Bernard Systems International, April 23-25, 1980.

84   The capacity of the system: Angell, William M. "Material Handling Classics." Small Parts Orderpicking, 1980 Automated Material Handling Storage Systems Conference. Clay Bernard Systems International, April 23-25, 1980.

85   The video footage shown: ABC-News. ABC, October 6, 1982. -- *ABC Nightline*, ABC, October 1, 1982.

85   The 165,000 stores that sold Tylenol nationwide: Reis, Al; Trout, Jack. *Marketing Warfare*. New York City: The McGraw Hill Companies, 2006, Pg. 62.

86   Zahn Drug served 1,400 drugstores: Associated Press. "Hearing for two accused in kidnap delayed two days." *Winona Daily News*, July 3, 1973.

86   The company had formed a network: "Medical info card available." *Forrest Park Review*, October 12, 1977, p19. -- "Drug store joins network." *The Herald*, December 12, 1974.

86   The Family Drug Center (FDC) stores were located: "Medical info card available." *Forrest Park Review*, October 12, 1977, p19. -- "Zahn Drug links with Familycare." *The Daily Herald*, August 24, 1981.

86   On the morning Johnson & Johnson: Maroney, David. "Logan Shelves Being Emptied." *Pharos Tribune*, October 1, 1982.

86   "People started calling": Maroney, David. "Logan Shelves Being Emptied." *Pharos Tribune*: October 1, 1982

87   The urgent calls from McNeil: Maroney, David. "Logan Shelves Being Emptied." *Pharos Tribune*, October 1, 1982.

87   Chicago pharmacist, Robert Wijas: *ABC World News Tonight*. ABC, October 6, 1982.

88   On Saturday, October 2nd, Fahner said investigators: Associated Press. "Byrne bans sale of all Tylenol in the big city." *Sunday Roswell Daily Record*, October 3, 1982.

88   On October 1st, officials from the Tylenol task force: "Tylenol Contamination." *Nightline*. ABC, October 1, 1982.

88   "We've had the Illinois Department of Law Enforcement": *ABC World News Tonight*. ABC, October 6, 1982.

89   At that time, the only two bottles of cyanide-laced Tylenol recovered so far had been purchased at the Jewel-Osco stores: Beck, Melinda; Hagar, Mary; LaBreque, Ron; Monroe, Sylvester; Prout, Linda. "The Tylenol Scare." Newsweek, October 11, 1982.

88   Zahn Drug was acquired by FoxMeyer: McKesson Plants to Add FoxMeyer Health unit." The New York Times, October 5, 1996. -- "Drug company acquires Zahn." The Daily Herald, August 27, 1988.

89   McKesson was the sole supplier of pharmaceuticals to Jewel-Osco: McKesson Corp. "McKesson, American Drug Stores ink supply management pact." July 20, 1998. Accessed   January,   11   2011. http://www.mckesson.com/en_us/McKesson.com/About%2BUs/Newsroom/Newsroom.html

89   McKesson is also the current pharmacy service provider for Central DuPage Hospital: "A Multi-Vendor Approach to Restructuring Medication Management Systems," *Pharmacy Purchasing & Products*, January 2008, Vol. 5, No. 1.

16   The Plot Thickens

91   On Wednesday, October 6, 1982: USA, Plaintiff-Appellee, v. James William Lewis, Defendant-Appellant. No. 84-2011. US Court of Appeals, Seventh Circuit, May 31, 1985.

91   Seven days after: "Cyanide-Tylenol Extortion Hoax Suspect Was Indicted for Murder." *Syracuse Post Standard*, October 15, 1982.

91   James and his wife: Lewis, James. Email interview by author, re: Aljeev International, July 31, 2010. -- Bergmann, Joy. "A Bitter Pill." *Chicago Reader*, November 3, 2000.

92   When the Tylenol murders made front-page: USA, Plaintiff-Appellee, v. James William Lewis, Defendant-Appellant. No. 84-2011. US Court of Appeals, Seventh Circuit, May 31, 1985.

92   Tyrone Fahner downplayed the significance: "Chicago Officials Check Wyoming Cyanide Death." Tyrone *Daily Herald*, October 9, 1982. -- Associated Press. "Tylenol makers report $1 million extortion plot." *Alton Telegraph*, October 8, 1982.

92   On Friday, October 8, 1982: Malcolm, Andrew H. "Wyoming cyanide death investigated." *The New York Times*, October 9, 1982.

93   Sheridan County Coroner Jim Kane said the capsules weren't suspected: Associated Press. "Tylenol suspected in Unsolved Cyanide Death in Wyoming," *Syracuse Post Standard*, October 9, 1982.

93   Dr. William Doughty: Malcolm, Andrew H. "Wyoming cyanide death investigated." *The New York Times*, October 9, 1982.

93   Doughty asked the manager: Malcolm, Andrew H. "Wyoming cyanide death investigated." *The New York Times*, October 9, 1982.

93   A second analysis: Malcolm, Andrew H. "Wyoming cyanide death investigated." *The New York Times*, October 9, 1982.

93   "It turned out,": Malcolm, Andrew H. "Wyoming cyanide death investigated." *The New York Times*, October 9, 1982.

94   When the Chicago detective: Associated Press. "Cyanide probe narrowed to 3 or 4 primary leads." The Galveston Daily News, October 11, 1982.

94   In addition to the cyanide: Madrzyk, Anna; Gores, Paul. "Cyanide Killer Search Widens." *The Sunday Herald*, October 3, 1982.

94   Acetaminophen is second only: Ionescu, DN; Janssen, JK; Omalu. "Final Diagnosis -- Acute Combined Drug Overdose of Ethanol, Acetaminophen, Imipramine, Desipramine, Oxycodone and Diphenhydramine," University of Pennsylvania School of   Pathology   website.   Accessed   July   20,   2011. http://path.upmc.edu/cases/case407/dx.html

95   On January 13, 1983: "Drug death probes reopened." *The Daily Herald*: January 13, 1983

95   "We are continuing these investigations": "Drug death probes reopened." *The Daily Herald*, January 13, 1983.

95   Cook County medical examiners found acetaminophen (Tylenol) and lethal levels of cyanide: United Press International. "Excedrin removed from Colorado stores." *The Hutchinson News*, October 27, 1982.

96   Yet Jaye Schroeder, a Chicago police spokesperson: United Press International. "Excedrin removed from Colorado stores." The Hutchinson News, October 27, 1982.

96   Dr. Mitra Kalelkar, the Assistant Medical Examiner: "Early Cyanide Death Not Tied to Tylenol, Authorities Believe." New York Times, October 28, 1982.

96   Husted and Louis Tedesco: United States of America, Plaintiff-appellee, v. Louis Tedesco, Defendant-appellant. United States Court of Appeals, Seventh Circuit. - 726 F.2d 1216,

96   Husted had flown to Chicago: Mark Husted family members. Telephone interview by author, February 16, 2010.

96   Tedesco told police: "Federal agents probe death of drug dealer." *The Daily Herald*, September 17, 1982.

96   Agents from the DEA: "Federal agents probe death of drug dealer." *The Daily Herald*, September 17, 1982.

97   "a feeling that his son may have been murdered.": "Federal agents probe death of drug dealer." *The Daily Herald*, September 17, 1982.

97   "Ate Tylenol like candy:: Mark Husted family members. Telephone interview by author, February 16, 2010.

17   A Poisoned Investigation

99   By October 9, 1982, Cook County: United Press International. "Suspect List Cut to Four." *Pharos-Tribune*, October 10, 1982.

99   Cook County Toxicologist, Michael Schaffer, said the cyanide: Beck, Melinda; Hagar, Mary; LaBreque, Ron; Monroe, Sylvester; Prout, Linda. "The Tylenol Scare." *Newsweek*, October 11, 1982.

99   On October 21, 1982, a J&J employee: United Press International. "More Poisoned Tylenol Discovered In Chicago." *Pharos-Tribune*, October 22, 1982.

100   "advanced state of deterioration": Cialini, Joe. "Death from cyanide linked to Tylenol." *The Progress*, October 7, 1982. -- Malcolm, Andrew H. "Another poisoned Tylenol bottle is found by Chicago investigators." *The New York Times*, October 22, 1982.

100   To find out when and where: Associated Press. "Suspects Studied in Cyanide Deaths." *Casa Grande Dispatch*, October 4, 1982.

100   He said that after the cyanide had been in the test capsules for 48 hours: Litke, James. "Cyanide kills Philadelphian." *The Gettysburg Times*, October 7, 1982.

100   On October 9, 1982, Stein said: United Press International. "Suspect List Cut to Four." *Pharos-Tribune*, October 10, 1982.

100   Instead of acknowledging the relevance of Stein's findings, Fahner sharply criticized: United Press International. "Suspect List Cut to Four." *Pharos-Tribune*, October 10, 1982.

101   "The Illinois Department of Law Enforcement, the FBI": Lewis, James. ABC-7 Personal Interview by Chuck Goudie, 1992.

101   On October 8, 1982, NBC-News showed video footage: *Nightly News*. NBC, October 8, 1982.

101   Tyrone Fahner said the cyanide-laced Tylenol: Rutenberg, Sharon. "More Than One 'Madman' Tylenol Killer is Hinted." *The Progress*, October 4, 1982.

102   The chemical makeup: Doyle, Pat. "A year after Tylenol killings: sorrow lingers, answers elude." *The Sunday Herald*, September 25, 1983.

102   The FDA traced the cyanide to DuPont: The Ames Lab: Creating Materials and Energy   Solutions.   "Did   you   know"   brochure. https://www.ameslab.gov/files/DidYouKnowThat_0.pdf

102   The *Chicago Tribune* reported that the poisoned Tylenol capsules contained: Associated Press. "Cyanide source to be probed." *The Galveston Daily News*, November 13, 1982.

102   In early 1986, the FDA conducted its own analysis of cyanide-laced Tylenol capsules: Norman, Michael. "FBI is assigning Tylenol inquiry 'highest priority.'" *The New York Times*, February 15, 1986.

18   A Shelf-life Problem

103   The Tylenol Monograph: "Tylenol Professional Product Information." Tylenol website, 2010. Accessed June 20, 2011. http://www.tylenolprofessional.com/assets/TYL_PPI.pdf

103   The source of the stability data: Fairbrother J. Acetaminophen. New York, NY: Academic Press; 1974.

103   Dean Mickelson, a pharmacist: "Pharmacies pull drug," *The Taos News*: Oct 7, 1982.

103   Forty months later, in February 1986: Inquirer Wire Service (with contribution from Michael B. Coakley). "Cyanide in Tylenol; Woman Dead." *Inquirer*, February 11, 1986.

103   Oddly, all of the Tylenol involved: Coleman, Brenda. "FDA advises against use of Extra-Strength Tylenol." *Alton Telegraph*, October 1, 1982. – United Press International. "Laced Tylenol claims 7th; culprit unknown." Pacific Stars and Stripes, October 4, 1982. -- Associated Press. "More Poison: 8th tainted bottle found." *New Braunfels Herald-Zeitung*, October 26, 1982.

103   The Tylenol from Lot MC2880: "Three Die After Taking Cyanide-Tainted Tylenol." The Harvard Crimson website, October 1, 1982. Accessed July 1, 2011. http://www.thecrimson.com/article/1982/10/1/three-die-after-taking-cyanide-tainted-tylenol/?print=1. -- 10 p.m. News. WMAQ-TV, NBC, Chicago, October 1, 1982.

104   The Tylenol from Lot 1910MD: Associated Press. "Poison Found in Another Tylenol Batch." *Winchester Star*, October 1, 1982. -- 10 p.m. News. WMAQ-TV, NBC, Chicago, October 1, 1982.

104   was manufactured between January and May of 1982: A.P. "R.P. halts Extra-Strength Tylenol sales, imports," *Pacific Stars and Stripes*, October 7, 1982.

104   An FOIA request was filed with the FDA: Konigstein, David. Response to FOIA Request, File 2011-4678, July 26, 2011.

104   In 1973, the DOD: "SLEP - The DoD/FDA Shelf Life Extension Program." Accessed July 10, 2011. https://slep.dmsbfda.army.mil/portal/page/portal/SLEP_PAGE_GRP/SLEP_HOME_NEW

104   On July 1, 1975, the FDA: "MOU 224-76-8049: Memorandum of Understanding Between The Veterans Administration and The Food and Drug Administration." June 12, 1975.

105   Throughout the 1980s, the DOD: DOD Contract with McNeil Consumer Products Company, Round Rock, Texas, Contract number LA12082 C0776, May 1982. – DOD

(Air force) Contract with McNeil Consumer Products Co., Glendale, California, Contract number SA13H 77 50158, Fiscal year 1980.

105   At the time of the Tylenol murders: United Press International. "Kansans told not to use Tylenol." *Salina Journal*, October 3, 1982.

105   "We're yanking it.": Associated Press. "Extra Strength Tylenol off shelves in Kansas." *The Iola Register*, October 2, 1982.

105   Public Affairs Officer, Jane Wray: United Press International. "Kansans told not to use Tylenol." *Salina Journal*, October 3, 1982.

105   Air Force officials discovered: Trimmer, Dwight. "Refunds Offered on Tylenol Products." *Pacific Stars and Stripes*, October 15, 1982.

105   Drug diversion was a big problem: GAO. "FOOD AND DRUG ADMINISTRATION HHS Inspector General Should Be Involved in Criminal Investigations." Report to the Subcommittee on Oversight and Investigations, Committee on Energy and Commerce, House of Representatives, November 1987. – Associated Press. "7 Ohio drug companies being probed." *Chronicle-Telegram*, September 16, 1985.

105   Diverters actively sought out: Associated Press. "'Drug diversion' is $1B business." *Pacific Stars and Stripes*, August 10, 1985. -- Associated Press. "'Shadow' drug market detailed." 1986. -- Kenyon, Quane. "Drugs Worth $380,000 On Street Missing AtSHS." *Idaho State Journal*, October 30, 1977.

105   According to a March 19, 1982 GAO report: GAO. "Review of Prices Paid by Military Commissaries on Brand Name Vendor Supply Bulletin Contracts (PLRD-82-55)." March 19, 1982.

106   They said the Tylenol was packaged: Associated Press. "Cyanide found in another Tylenol batch." *The Paris News*, October 1, 1982.

106   J&J spokesperson Marshall Molloy said McNeil: Associated Press. "Sixth Victim Claimed By Cyanide Pills." *Bedford Gazette*, October 2, 1982.

106   It was the headquarters of the R. W. Johnson: McNeil Pharmaceutical. "McNeil Pharmaceutical Company; SUPROL Brand Suprofen; 6505-00D001599." DrugBank website. December 4, 1986. Accessed July 20, 2011 http://www.drugbank.ca/system/msds/DB00870.pdf?1265922742. – Reynolds, Brian E. "McNEil Pharmaceutical Div. of McNeil Labs Inc. -- HALDOL Brand Haloperidol Tablets; 10 MG; 6505-01-048-8982." Vermont Safety Information Resources website, November 21, 1985. Accessed July 20, 2011. http://hazard.com/msds/f2/bgh/bghxx.html . -- Reitz, Allen. "About the Cover." ACS Publications website, March 11, 1991. Accessed July 22, 2011. http://pubs.acs.org/doi/pdf/10.1021/bk-1991-0463.pr001 . -- Allen Reitz Biography on Planet Connect website. Accessed July 22, 2011. http://events.planetconnect.com/careerworkshopprogram.html

107   Large fiber drums containing Tylenol: "When it Really Hurts." Tylox advertisement, on NCBI website 1986. Accessed July 22, 2011. http://www.ncbi.nlm.nih.gov/pmc/articles/PMC1251264/pdf/annsurg00091-0002.pdf

19   We Know Who Did It

109   During the first few days: Associated Press. "Cyanide is Discovered in Tylenol in an April Death in Philadelphia." *The New York Times*, October 7, 1982.

109   On Tuesday, October 5th: United Press International. "Philadelphia Cyanide Link Not Solid: Top Investigator." *Pharos-Tribune*, October 7, 1982.

109   "the list of suspects has been narrowed":   United Press International. "Philadelphia Cyanide Link Not Solid: Top Investigator." Pharos-Tribune, October 7, 1982.

109   On October 9th, Fahner, anxious: United Press International. "Tylenol poisoning probe narrowed to 4 suspects." *Pacific Stars and Stripes*, October 11, 1982.

109   By the end of that same day: Associated Press. "Cyanide probe narrowed down to just a few leads." *Wisconsin State Journal*, October 11, 1982.

109   Fahner said six prime suspects: "Chicago lie tests clear 6." Chicago Sun Times, October 27, 1982.

110   "Me and my gang put cyanide in every bottle":   Associated Press. "No progress made in Tylenol deaths." *The Gettysburg Press*, October 12, 1982.

110   Howard, a 20-year-old: United Press International. "Chicago man hit for extortion; laced Tylenol link is ruled out." *Pacific Stars and Stripes*, October 12, 1982.

110   "There is no credible": Associated Press. "No progress made in Tylenol deaths." *The Gettysburg Press*, October 12, 1982.

110   Fahner said the Howard case: United Press International. "Chicago man hit for extortion; laced Tylenol link is ruled out." *Pacific Stars and Stripes*, October 12, 1982.

110   Police believe the poisoned capsules: *Nightly News*. NBC, October 8, 1982.

110   "This is the case that does not": *Nightly News*. NBC, October 8, 1982.

111   The Winfield police will not confirm: Watkins, Scott. Personal Interview by author, August 19, 2010. - Watkins, Scott. Personal interview by Michelle Rosen, March 12, 2010. – Bellisario, Frank. Personal interview by Michelle Rosen, March 2010. – Samuels, Sharon. FOIA request reply, June 16, 2011.

111   However, on March 9, 2010: Watkins, Scott. Personal Interview by author, August 19, 2010.

112   "We know who did it.": Associated Press. "Report says investigators know identity of Tylenol murderer." *Alton Telegraph*, March 10, 1983.

20   The Closet Chemist

113   On Saturday evening, October 9th: "Why Tylenol deaths might go unsolved." *The Daily Herald,* September 29, 2002. -- Associated Press. "Cyanide suspect once indicted for murder." *Galveston Daily News*, October 15, 1982. -- Chicago Police Detective. Confidential telephone interview by author, February 5, 2009.

113   The tavern's owner, Marty Sinclair: "Cyanide-Tylenol Extortion Hoax Suspect Was Indicted for Murder." *Syracuse Post Standard*, October 15, 1982. -- Chicago Detective on 1982 Tylenol task force. Confidential phone interview by author, February 5, 2009.

113   Two days later, Arnold was in Lilly's Bar: Petition for Executive Clemency in Behalf of Roger Arnold, Cook County Circuit Court, 1996 -- Associated Press. "Man Questioned in Cyanide Deaths." *Dispatch*, October 13, 1982. -- "Police Search Home Of Tylenol Suspect." *Daily Sitka Sentinel*, October 14, 1982.

113   Arnold later said authorities: "Rush for Justice, Lifetime of Regret." *Chicago Sun-Times*, March 3, 1996.

113   Roger Arnold was born: Petition for Executive Clemency in Behalf of Roger Arnold. Cook County Circuit Court, 1996.

114   In 1969, Arnold took a job: Petition for Executive Clemency in Behalf of Roger Arnold. Cook County Circuit Court, 1996. -- Associated Press. "Man Questioned in Cyanide Deaths." *Dispatch*, October 13, 1982.

114   Prior to the aggravated assault charge: Petition for Executive Clemency in Behalf of Roger Arnold. Cook County Circuit Court, 1996.

114   Chicago Police Detective James Gildea: Associated Press. "Police Search Suspect's Home Again After Release on Bond." *Dispatch*, October 14, 1982.

114   On Tuesday afternoon, Chicago police detectives: Blum, Howard. "It was a Typical Night for the Tylenol Task Force." *The New York Times*, October 15, 1982.

114   "You can read": Blum, Howard. "It was a Typical Night for the Tylenol Task Force." *The New York Times*, October 15, 1982.

115   Jewel, with more than: "Hospital association gets $50,000 gift," *Economist Newspapers*, November 16, 1977.

115   "At first [Arnold] denied": 10 p.m. News. NBC, WMAQ-TV: October 13, 1982.

115   "[Arnold] dropped the comment": 10 p.m. News. NBC, WMAQ-TV: October 13, 1982.

115   "I want you: Blum, Howard. "It was a Typical Night for the Tylenol Task Force." *The New York Times*, October 15, 1982.

115   Arnold had married Delores in 1970: Petition for Executive Clemency in Behalf of Roger Arnold. Cook County Circuit Court, 1996.

115   The divorce was finalized in July of 1982: Blum, Howard. "It was a Typical Night for the Tylenol Task Force." *The New York Times*, October 15, 1982.

115   Delores could not believe: Blum, Howard. "It was a Typical Night for the Tylenol Task Force." *The New York Times*, October 15, 1982.

116   Detectives Eddy and Rebholz finished: Blum, Howard. "It was a Typical Night for the Tylenol Task Force." *The New York Times*, October 15, 1982.

116   While searching Arnold's house: United Press International: "More Poisoned Tylenol found." *Tyrone Daily*, October 26, 1982. -- "Police Search Suspect's Home Again After Release on Bond." *Dispatch*, October 14, 1982.

116   Arnold's reading material included: Nightly News. NBC, October 13, 1982. -- Associated Press. "Police question 'chemist' in cyanide-deaths case." *The New Mexican*, October 13, 1982.

116   Police found lab equipment and various chemicals: Chicago Police Detective. Phone interview by author, February 5, 2009.

116   a large amount of a certain type of hair-gel used in making homemade bombs: Chicago Detective on Tylenol task force. Confidential telephone interview by Scott Bartz, February 5, 2009.

116   Police also turned up a suspicious-looking: Wire Service. "'Unrelated' arrests made in Tylenol death case." *Pacific Stars and Stripes*, October 15, 1982.

116   A spokesperson for the Chicago police later said: "More Headaches." *TIME*, October 25, 1982.

117   Arnold was held without bond: Associated Press. "Police Search Home of Tylenol Suspect." *Daily Sitka Sentinel*, October 14, 1982.

117   Lieutenant Locallo said a "series of coincidences": "Cyanide-Tylenol Extortion Hoax Suspect Was Indicted for Murder." *Syracuse Post Standard*, October 15, 1982.

117   The reported these coincidences: Associated Press. "Police Search Home of Tylenol Suspect." *Daily Sitka Sentinel*, October 14, 1982.

117   According to the *Daily Herald*, Arnold: "Why Tylenol deaths might go unsolved." *The Daily Herald*, September 29, 2002.

117   Arnold was released: United Press International. "Cyanide Suspect Released on Bail." *Tyrone Daily Herald*, October 14, 1982.

117   Chicago Police Detective Jerry Beam: Associated Press. "Man Questioned in Cyanide Deaths." *Dispatch*, October 13, 1982.

117   "It doesn't appear the man": Wire Service. "'Unrelated' arrests made in Tylenol death case." *Pacific Stars and Stripes*: October 15, 1982.

117   Nevertheless, when Arnold was released from jail: Associated Press. "Eighth Poisoned Bottle Of Tylenol Discovered." *Daily News Record*, October 26, 1982.

117   Arnold's lawyer, Thomas Royce: Goudie, Chuck; Pistone, Ann. "Legendary Chicago defense lawyer dies at 64." ABC-local website, October 6, 2009. Accessed, July 20, 2011. http://abclocal.go.com/wls/story?section=news/iteam&id=7051285

117   Surveillance was so heavy, said Royce: McNamee, Tom. Rush for Justice, Lifetime of Regret." *Chicago Sun-Times*, March 3, 1996.

117   The reading material confiscated: United Press International. "Cyanide suspect freed on bond." *Altoona Mirror*, October 14, 1982.

117   Arnold said he went to Thailand: United Press International. "Cyanide suspect freed on bond." *Altoona Mirror*, October 14, 1982.

118   "They can say what they want": United Press International. "Cyanide Suspect Released on Bail." *Tyrone Daily Herald*, October 14, 1982.

118   "I was willing to take a polygraph": United Press International. "Cyanide suspect freed on bond." *Altoona Mirror*, October 14, 1982.

118   "I knew the family": United Press International. "Cyanide suspect freed on bond." *Altoona Mirror*, October 14, 1982.

118   Fahner described Arnold's arrest: Associated Press. "Man Questioned in Cyanide Deaths." *Dispatch*, October 13, 1982.

21   A Conspiracy Theory

119   On Friday, October 22nd: *Nightly News*, NBC: October 25, 1982.

119   Howard Fearon, Sr., the father: "6 Cyanide murders cover for seventh?" *Ironwood Daily Globe*, October 25, 1982. -- Associated Press "Tylenol victim's relative a suspect." *Marysville Journal*, October 25, 1982. – Associated Press. "Tylenol victim's relative a suspect." *Register*, October 25, 1982.

119   On Monday evening: *Nightly News*, NBC: October 25, 1982.

120   "drinking buddies": United Press International. "More Cyanide-Laced Tylenol Found; Colorado Incidents Investigated." *The Progress*, October 26, 1982.

120   Investigators had evidently: Associated Press. "Kansas City slaying kinked to man sought in Tylenol questioning." *The Register*, October 15, 1982. -- United Press International. "More Cyanide-Laced Tylenol Found; Colorado Incidents Investigated." *The Progress*, October 26, 1982. -- Associated Press. Tylenol Victim's Kin Is Suspect." *The Winchester Star*, October 25, 1982.

120   "I knew the family: United Press International. "Cyanide suspect freed on bond." *Altoona Mirror*, October 14, 1982.

120   On Monday, October 25th, NBC reported: *Nightly News*. NBC, October 25, 1982.

120   "He is the most innocent person": The News Service. "Prime Suspect in Tylenol Case Passes Lie Detector Test." *Winnipeg Free Press*, October 27, 1982.

120   "Chicago authorities now believe they know the real story": *Nightly News*. NBC, October 25, 1982.

121   "Investigators now believe the seven Tylenol murders": *Nightly News*. NBC, October 25, 1982.

121   "members of the family of Mrs. Reiner": Litke, James. "Eighth bottle of Tainted Tylenol is discovered." *Chillicothe Constitution-Tribune*, October 26, 1982.

121   NBC showed video footage of an unidentified: *Nightly News*. NBC, October 25, 1982

121   The unmarked vehicle shown in the NBC video footage was actually parked outside the home of Ed Reiner: Reiner, Ed. Personal interview by author. Winfield, IL, May 22, 2010. – Rosen, Michelle. Personal interview by author, May 22, 2010.

121   The prime suspect referenced by Tom Brokaw: Reiner, Ed. Personal interview by author. Winfield, IL, May 22, 2010.

121   Ed wasn't home when NBC: Reiner, Ed. Personal interview by author. Winfield, IL, May 22, 2010.

121   IDLE investigators asked Ed: Reiner, Ed. Personal interview by author. Winfield, IL, May 22, 2010.

122   The interrogation of Reiner: Litke, James. "Woman turns in bottle of tainted Tylenol." *Sequin Gazette-Enterprise*, October 26, 1982 -- Personal interview by author. Winfield, IL, May 22, 2010.

122   An IDLE investigator began: Reiner, Ed. Personal interview by author. Winfield, IL, May 22, 2010.

122   Reiner was flabbergasted: Reiner, Ed. Reiner, Ed. Personal interview by author. Winfield, IL, May 22, 2010.

122   In a condescending, perverse tone: Reiner, Ed. Personal interview by author. Winfield, IL, May 22, 2010.

123   To the consternation of his attorney: Reiner, Ed. Personal interview by author. Winfield, IL, May 22, 2010.

22   The Eighth Bottle

125   "Investigators say that since the negotiations": *NBC-News*, NBC: October 25, 1982.

125   The eighth bottle: United Press International: "More Poisoned Tylenol found." *Tyrone Daily*, October 26, 1982.

125   The cyanide-laced capsules in the eighth bottle: Litke, James. "Police Seek Woman Who Turned in Tylenol." *The Galveston Daily News*, October 27, 1982.

125   On Monday night, a law enforcement source: United Press International: "More Poisoned Tylenol found." *Tyrone Daily*, October 26, 1982.

126   The source said the woman: Associated Press. "More Tainted Tylenol Found in Chicago." *Syracuse Post-Standard*, October 26, 1982.

126   The Maple Plain Company was handling the reverse distribution: Associated Press. "Coupon company hired for Tylenol swap." *Gazette*, October 8, 1982.

126   "In response to this rapidly changing situation": Gates, Thomas N. "McNeil Consumer Products Co. 'Dear Doctor' Letter": signed by Dr. Thomas N. Gates, October 13, 1982.

127   In a statement Monday night: Associated Press. "More Tainted Tylenol Found in Chicago." *Syracuse Post-Standard*, October 26, 1982.

127   The next day, however, Wheaton Police: Associated Press. "Woman Who Turned in Tainted Tylenol is Sought." *The New York Times*, October 27, 1982.

127   "definitely said she": Associated Press. "Woman Who Turned in Tainted Tylenol is Sought." *The New York Times*, October 27, 1982.

127   When the FBI interviewed: Litke, James. "Police Seek Woman Who Turned in Tylenol." *The Galveston Daily News*, October 27, 1982.

127   "We don't know": Litke, James. "Police Seek Woman Who Turned in Tylenol." *The Galveston Daily News*, October 27, 1982.

128   On Wednesday afternoon, the woman: United Press International. "Fingerprint Found On Tainted Tylenol Bottle." *The Progress*, October 28, 1982.

128   Wheaton Police Chief: United Press International. "Fingerprint Found On Fainted Tylenol Bottle." *The Progress*, October 28, 1982.

128   "I believe now": United Press International. "Fingerprint discovered on poison Tylenol." *Hutchinson News*, October 28, 1982.

128   Fahner held a news conference on Wednesday: United Press International. "Print Found On Tylenol Box May Not Aid Probe." *Pharos-Tribune*, October 28, 1982. -

- P-S Wire Service. "FBI Finds Fingerprint on Tylenol Box." *The Post-Standard*, October 28, 1982.

128 "closer than we have ever been": United Press International. "Chicago Officials Closer to Tylenol Case Arrest." *Pharos Tribune*, October 27, 1982.

128 "I opened the capsule": United Press International. "New Tylenol-Cyanide Mix Found." *Pharos-Tribune*, Oct 29, 1982.

129 According to Tyrone Fahner, the cyanide-laced capsules: Associated Press. "Official: More than one may be responsible for poisonings." *The Register*, October 29, 1982. -- Associated Press. "Latest capsule has differences." *The Lethbridge Herald*: October 29, 1982.

129 "Some [cyanide-laced capsules in the eighth bottle] were put together unartfully.": Associated Press. "Official: More than one may be responsible for poisonings." *The Register*, October 29, 1982.

129 The condition of the shells: Associated Press. "Latest capsule has differences." *The Lethbridge Herald*, October 29, 1982.

129 "swollen and discolored": Beck, Melinda; Hagar, Mary; LaBreque, Ron; Monroe, Sylvester; Prout, Linda. "The Tylenol Scare." *Newsweek*, October 11, 1982.

129 "advanced state of deterioration": Malcolm, Andrew H. "Another poisoned Tylenol bottle is found by Chicago investigators." *The New York Times*, October 22, 1982.

129 Fahner said the seven cyanide-laced Tylenol capsules in the eighth bottle: Associated Press. "Official: More than one may be responsible for poisonings." *The Register*, October 29, 1982. -- Associated Press. "Latest capsule has differences." *The Lethbridge Herald*: October 29, 1982. -- Associated Press. "Second Poisoner Pondered." *Chronicle-Telegram*, October 29, 1982.

129 The FBI said they never found a match: United Press International. "FBI Can't Match Fingerprint on Tylenol Bottle." *Altoona Mirror*, October 29, 1982.

23   The Conspiracy

131 "Investigators think Winfield may not have been chosen at random: *Nightly News*. NBC, October 8, 1982.

132 ...but the Tylenol in the eighth bottle of cyanide-laced Tylenol was manufactured: "Three Die After Taking Cyanide-Tainted Tylenol." *The Harvard Crimson* website, October 1, 1982. Accessed July 1, 2011. -- 10 p.m. News. WMAQ-TV, NBC, October 1, 1982. – *Nightly News*, NBC, October 8, 1982.

132 An investigation completed by J&J: Coroner's inquest, re: Lynn Reiner, direct examination by DuPage County Coroner Richard Ballinger, 1982. Watkins, Scott. Personal Interview by author, August 19, 2010. -- Dependable Distribution Centers: Family Owned Business Built on a 'Dependable' Foundation: Hernandez, Vincint, *Recharger Magazine*, February, 2006.

134 The *Chicago Sun-Times* reported on October 26th that: The News Service. "Prime Suspect in Tylenol Case Passes Lie Detector Test." *Winnipeg Free Press*, October 27, 1982.

134   When Linda Morgan: United Press International. "Fingerprint Found On Tainted Tylenol Bottle." *The Progress*, October 28, 1982.

134   DuPage County Sheriff's detectives working on the Nicarico: Sevener, Donald. "A Capital Blunder." *Chicago Reader*, July 27, 1989. -- Possley, Maurice; Armstrong, Ken. "Prosecution on trial in DuPage." *Chicago Tribune*, January 12, 1999.

135   In the 1980s and 1990s: Warden, Rob. "Illinois Death Penalty Reform: How it Happened, What it Promises." The Journal of Criminal Law and Criminology. Northwestern University, School of Law, 2005.

135   The Illinois Governor's Commission: Randall, Kate. "Law and order in Illinois— frame-up, torture and legal murder." World Socialist Web Site, January 23, 2003. Accessed July 1, 2011. http://www.wsws.org/articles/2003/jan2003/ill-j23.shtml

136   "He [Fahner] probably had: McNamee, Tom. "Rush for Justice, Lifetime of Regret." *Chicago Sun-Times*, March 3, 1996.

136   Officials from the Tylenol task force: "Letter to the Stockholders," in Johnson & Johnson 1982 Annual Report, 1983.

136   Fahner said the prints on those capsules from were smudged: United Press International. "FBI Can't Match Fingerprint on Tylenol Bottle." *Altoona Mirror*, October 29, 1982.

136   The sixth bottle: Madrzyk, Anna; Gores, Paul. "Cyanide Killer Search Widens." *The Sunday Herald*: October 3, 1982.

137   Officials initially said they found two: Malcolm, Andrew H. "Search for the Tylenol Killer: Many Clues, But No Solution." *The New York Times*, October 10, 1982. -- Associated Press. "7th Chicago-area death blamed on poisoned drug." *The News*, October 2, 1982. -- Associated Press. "Madman's Plot Suspected; More Tainted Tylenol Found." *The News Record*, October 2, 1982.

137   FDA Deputy Director Mark Novitch later confirmed: Novitch, Mark, "Tylenol: The Granddady of Crisis," in *Communicating in a Healthcare Crisis*, ed. Pines, Wayne L. 183-186, Church Falls: FDAnews, 2007.

137   "No Reiner family member is a suspect": United Press International. "Chicago Officials Closer To Tylenol Case Arrest." *Pharos Tribune*, October 27, 1982.

24   The Last Suspect

139   Authorities, by clearing Associated Press. "Suspect in Tylenol case wanted to settle grudge." *Alton Telegraph*, November 5, 1982.

139   "Now is the time": Associated Press. "Suspect in Tylenol case wanted to settle grudge." *Alton Telegraph*, November 5, 1982.

139   The reference to Frank's Finer: Associated Press. "Cyanide suspect held grudge against two grocery stores." *The Lethbridge Herald*, November 4, 1982.

139   The manager of Frank's Finer Foods in Wheaton: Associated Press. "Suspect in Tylenol case wanted to settle grudge." *Alton Telegraph*, November 5, 1982.

139   An affidavit filed in the 18th Circuit Court: Associated Press. "New suspect sought in Tylenol murders." *The Capital*, November 2, 1982.

139   Jewel Vice President, Jane Armstrong, confirmed that the woman had filed: Associated Press. "Suspect in Tylenol case wanted to settle grudge." *Alton Telegraph*, November 5, 1982.

140   "I feel he [Kevin] was used": Constable, Burt. "Masterson: suspect or victim?" *The Sunday Herald*, October 2, 1983.

140   "The injustice done was so gross": Constable, Burt. "Masterson: suspect or victim?" *The Sunday Herald*, October 2, 1983.

140   The Mastersons said their son: Constable, Burt. "Masterson: suspect or victim?" *The Sunday Herald*, October 2, 1983.

140   "There's still nothing to indicate Masterson is anything": Associated Press. "Suspect in Tylenol case wanted to settle grudge." *Alton Telegraph*, November 5, 1982.

140   Authorities didn't identify Lewis: Associated Press. "Tylenol suspect called dangerous." *The Iola Register*, October 16, 1982. -- "Cyanide-Tylenol Extortion Hoax Suspect Was Indicted for Murder." *Syracuse Post Standard*, October 15, 1982.

141   Thomas Royce said the postponement was a "delay tactic": "Chicago Officials Set To Crack Tylenol Case." *The Daily New*, October 27, 1982.

141   "I consider him a goof": United Press International. "2 arrested; not linked to Tylenol." *The Hawkeye*, October 13, 1982.

141   "I'd like to be in on the homicide": Bergmann, Joy. "A Bitter Pill." Chicago Reader, November 3, 2000. http://www.chicagoreader.com/chicago/tylenol-killings-a-bitter-pill/Content?oid=903786

141   On the morning of June 18: McNamee, Tom. "Rush for Justice, Lifetime of Regret." Chicago Sun-Times, March 3, 1996.

141   the two spoke briefly: Associated Press. "Ex-Tylenol suspect charged in murder." Pacific Stars and Stripes, June 22, 1982.

141   "I'm shot": Associated Press. "One-time Tylenol Suspect Indicted." *The Galveston Daily News*, June 21, 1983.

141   One of the witnesses: United Press International. "Former Tylenol suspect linked to fatal shooting." *The Sunday Herald*: June 19, 1983.

141   a Cook County Grand Jury: Associated Press. "One-time Tylenol Suspect Indicted." *The Galveston Daily News*, June 21, 1983.

141   Prosecutors for the Cook County State's: Associated Press. "One-time Tylenol Suspect Indicted." *The Galveston Daily News*, June 21, 1983.

141   They called the shooting a revenge murder: "Figure in Tylenol case guilty of slaying." *The Daily Herald*, January 12, 1984.

142   Royce denied that Arnold: United Press International. "Ex-Tylenol figure held in slaying." *Pharos-Tribune*, June 20, 1983.

142   After Arnold's arrest on October 11, 1982: Associated Press. "Police question 'chemist' in cyanide-deaths case." *The New Mexican*, October 13, 1982.

142   Four months prior to the Tylenol murders, Sinclair: Associated Press. "Police question 'chemist' in cyanide-deaths case." *The New Mexican*, October 13, 1982. --

McNamee, Tom. Rush for Justice, Lifetime of Regret." *Chicago Sun-Times*, March 3, 1996.

142   They had engaged in a conversation at Sinclair's bar: Chicago Detective on Tylenol task force. Confidential email Interview by author. February 5, 2009.

142   Sinclair knew Arnold well enough: McNamee, Tom. Rush for Justice, Lifetime of Regret." *Chicago Sun-Times*, March 3, 1996.

142   Arnold testified that Stanisha: McNamee, Tom. "Rush for Justice, Lifetime of Regret." *Chicago Sun-Times*, March 3, 1996.

143   In a nine-page synopsis: Marx, Gary; Mills, Steve. Tylenol case revisited. *Chicago Tribune*, February 8, 2009.

143   "One of the most": Bergmann, Joy. "A Bitter Pill." *Chicago Reader*, November 3, 2000.   http://www.chicagoreader.com/chicago/tylenol-killings-a-bitter-pill/Content?oid=903786

143   "a soldier of fortune type guy": United Press. "Cyanide Suspect Released On Bail." *Tyrone Daily*, October 14, 1982.

143   Arnold's literature included: *Nightly News*. NBC, October 13, 1982. -- Associated Press. "Police question 'chemist' in cyanide-deaths case." *The New Mexican*, October 13, 1982.

144   Just prior to the Tylenol: United Press International. "Police Arrest Suspect in Tylenol Case." *The Progress*: October 13, 1982 - Associated Press. "Man Questioned in Cyanide Deaths." *Dispatch*, October 13, 1982.

144   "Of course, the killer: Malcolm, Andrew H. "3 Years Later, Illinois is Still Trying to Solve Tylenol Deaths." *The New York Times*, February 21, 1986.

25   Project Chatham

145   *TIME* magazine, in its decade-ending: "Most Applauded Corporate Response to a Disaster." *TIME*, 1990, p. 81

145   "Within one year: Foster, Lawrence. "The Tylenol Tragedy: A Crime Without Precedent," in *Communicating in a Healthcare Crisis*, ed. Pines, Wayne L. 173-182, Church Falls: FDAnews, 2007.

146   J&J President David Clare: Foster, Lawrence. "The Tylenol Tragedy: A Crime Without Precedent," in *Communicating in a Healthcare Crisis*, ed. Pines, Wayne L. 173-182, Church Falls: FDAnews, 2007.

146   It was indeed fortunate: Moore, Thomas. "The Fight to Save Tylenol." *TIME*, November 29, 1982.

146   Johnson & Johnson had initiated "Project Chatham": Aguilar, Francis J.; Bhambri, Arvind: "Johnson & Johnson (B): Hospital Services." Harvard Business School Publishing, 1983.

146   Project Chatham sat dormant:: Aguilar, Francis J.; Bhambri, Arvind: "Johnson & Johnson (B): Hospital Services." Harvard Business School Publishing, 1983.

147   "I took some kidding at that meeting": Moore, Thomas. "The Fight to Save Tylenol." *TIME*, November 29, 1982.

147   The actions that followed: Novitch, Mark, "Tylenol: The Granddady of Crisis," in *Communicating in a Healthcare Crisis*, ed. Pines, Wayne L. 183-186, Church Falls: FDAnews, 2007.

148   Burke made up his mind Johnson & Johnson: "The Comeback" A Special Report from the Editors of Worldwide Publication of Johnson & Johnson Corporate Public Relations," 1982.

148   "It would almost": Atkinson, Rick. "The Tylenol Nightmare: How a Corporate Giant Fought Back." *The Kansas City Times*, November 12, 1982.

148   "We conclude that the contamination did not occur at either plant": United Press International. "FDA: Tylenol-maker blameless." *The Hutchinson News*, October 23, 1982.

149   Prior to re-launching Tylenol in tamper-resistant packaging: Moore, Thomas. "The Fight to Save Tylenol." *TIME*, November 29, 1982.

149   "We ran a series": Foster, Lawrence, interview by PSU students, 2002

149   "We want you": Minderovic, Christine Miner. "Tylenol Ad Campaign." Jiffynotes.com.
http://www.jiffynotes.com/a_study_guides/book_notes_add/emmc_0001_0001_0/e mmc_0001_0001_0_00177.html

149   In mid-November 1982:   Federal Drug Administration. "A Public Service announcement about over-the-counter medicine."   *The Galveston Daily News*, November 8, 1982.

149   Hayes said the poisonings were: Federal Drug Administration. "A Public Service announcement about over-the-counter medicine." *The Galveston Daily News*, November 8, 1982.

150   Larry Foster predicted that consumers: Associated Press. "Tylenol producers face big task." *Kokomo Tribune*, October 17, 1982.

150   *The New York Times* reported: Kleinfield, N.R. "Tylenol's Rapid Comeback." *New York Times*, September 17, 1983.

26   Legacy

151   *TIME* magazine, in its decade-ending: "Most Applauded Corporate Response to a Disaster." *TIME*, 1990, p. 81

151   Johnson & Johnson's response to the 1982 Tylenol: Yang, Jia Lynn. "Getting a handle on a scandal," *FORTUNE*, May 22, 2007.

151   An amicus brief filed in November 2002: O'Dwyer, Jack. "PR Industry's Amicus Brief   Has   a   Flaw."   ReclaimDemocracy.org
http://www.reclaimdemocracy.org/nike/pr_brief_retort_kasky_nike.html

151   The brief said, "Johnson & Johnson maintained an open dialogue": Nike Inc. et al. v. Marc Kasky. 02-575. U.S. Supreme Court, 2002.

152   Although it took about a week for J&J: O'Dwyer, Jack. "PR Industry's Amicus Brief   Has   a   Flaw."   Reclaim   Democracy   website,   November   19,   2002.
http://reclaimdemocracy.org/nike/pr_brief_retort_kasky_nike.html

152   Johnson & Johnson never held a press conference, but rather chose: O'Dwyer, Jack. "PR Industry's Amicus Brief Has a Flaw." ReclaimDemocracy.org http://www.reclaimdemocracy.org/nike/pr_brief_retort_kasky_nike.html

152   Yet Larry Foster said that amid the hysteria: Cooke, Jeremy R. "PSU alumnus recalls 1982 Tylenol murders." *Collegian*, October 18, 2002.

152   We couldn't be as open with them: Cooke, Jeremy R. "PSU alumnus recalls 1982 Tylenol murders." *Collegian*, October 18, 2002.

153   Product liability lawsuits were filed: Coleman, Brenda. "Poisoner's identity remains mystery after 6 months," *The Register*, March 27, 1983.

153   "Even if the Tylenol manufacturers had no knowledge: Associated Press. "Supreme court makes ruling in Tylenol case." *The Hawkeye*, December 22, 1987.

153   In January 1986, the lawsuits: Dennis Kellerman, Administrator, Petitioner v. Brian Crow, Judge, et al, No. 518 N,E. 2d, 116. Illinois Supreme Court, December 21, 1982.

153   "I foresee the cases going to trial": Associated Press. "Supreme court makes ruling in Tylenol case." *The Hawkeye*, December 22, 1987.

153   As the trial-date approached: Janota, Laura. "Tainted Tylenol Civil Case Will Begin." *Daily Herald*, May 13, 1991.

154   Late Saturday night, May 11: Carpenter, John; Gregory, Ted. "11th-hour deal closes Tylenol case." *The Daily Herald*, May 14, 1991.

154   Negotiations began immediately, with J&J's attorneys pressuring: Tylenol victims' relatives. Confidential interviews by author, 2010.

154   The secret settlement negotiations continued: Smith, Zay N. "Tylenol settlement - Kin of 7 dead to get millions in out-of-court agreement." *Chicago Sun-Times*, May 14, 1991.

154   Settlement agreements with all of the plaintiffs: Carpenter, John; Gregory, Ted. "11th-hour deal closes Tylenol case." *The Daily Herald*, May 14, 1991.

154   "The parties have resolved their differences": Smith, Zay N. "Tylenol settlement - Kin of 7 dead to get millions in out-of-court agreement." *Chicago Sun-Times*, May 14, 1991.

154   The plaintiffs and their lawyers: Associated Press. "After Tylenol case confidential settlements debated." *Daily Herald*, May 19, 1991. -- Szymczak, P. Davis. "Settlement Reached In Tylenol Suit." *Chicago Tribune*, May 14, 1991.

154   "No one can talk about that": Smith, Zay N. "Tylenol settlement - Kin of 7 dead to get millions in out-of-court agreement." *Chicago Sun-Times*, May 14, 1991.

154   According to the *Chicago Sun-Times*, "some estimates: Smith, Zay N. "Tylenol settlement - Kin of 7 dead to get millions in out-of-court agreement." *Chicago Sun-Times*, May 14, 1991.

154   Based on settlement information: Deyo, Russell. Confidential Tylenol Settlement Agreement, May 13, 1991. – Relatives of Tylenol murder victims. Confidential interviews by author, 2010.

154   "The public has a right to know about events": Associated Press. "After Tylenol case confidential settlements debated." *Daily Herald*, May 19, 1991.

155   "Though there is":   Janota, Laura. "Fear of negative publicity likely led to Tylenol settlement." *The Daily Herald*, May 15, 1991.

155   "They [J&J] saw their duty": Smith, Zay N. "Tylenol settlement - Kin of 7 dead to get millions in out-of-court agreement." *Chicago Sun-Times*, May 14, 1991.

155   "Liability will never again be brought": The New York Times News Service. "Tylenol lawsuit is settled before going to trial," *The Baltimore Sun*, May 14, 1991.

155   "It takes two to tango": Smith, Zay N. "Tylenol settlement - Kin of 7 dead to get millions in out-of-court agreement." *Chicago Sun-Times*, May 14, 1991.

Epilogue

157   "When all this is said and done": Coleman, Brenda. "Tylenol poisoner's identity remains mystery after 6 months." *The Register*, March 27, 1983.

157   "With Tylenol there was never a message": "Tylenol's "Miracle" Comeback: A year after the poisonings, public confidence is restored." *TIME*, October 17, 1983.

157   "The crime scenes": Griffin, Leslie. "One year later: Tylenol, Trauma recedes, search for killer goes on." *The Stars and Stripes*, August 21, 1983.

157   "There's just nothing": Griffin, Leslie. "One year later: Tylenol, Trauma recedes, search for killer goes on." *The Stars and Stripes*, August 21, 1983.

158   "Lewis remains the best": Burris, Anne. "5 years later, the Tylenol mystery remains." *Daily Herald*, September 30, 1987.

158   "Over the years, my position has been": Janota, Laura. "'Prime suspect' still maintains innocence." *Daily Herald*, September 27, 1992.

158   The FBI said new tips: Rice, Ross. "Media Advisory on Review of 1982 Tylenol Murders," FBI website, February 4, 2009. Accessed, July 20. 2011. www.FBI.gov . http://www.fbi.gov/chicago/press-releases/2009/feb04_09.htm